COMPANION PLANTING
for Beginners

Darren Sutton

COMPANION PLANTING FOR BEGINNERS

Table of Contents

Introduction to Companion Planting

Welcome to the enchanting world of companion gardening, a journey where plants become more than just solitary entities; they transform into partners, supporting and enhancing each other's growth. This book, is your gateway to understanding and embracing this beautiful, symbiotic relationship between plants.

In this introductory chapter, we'll explore the essence of companion gardening. It's a practice as ancient as agriculture itself, yet it holds renewed significance in our modern world. With an increasing focus on sustainable living and organic produce, companion gardening emerges not just as a hobby but as a meaningful step towards an eco-friendly lifestyle.

Whether you're a city dweller with a small balcony or a suburbanite with a modest backyard, companion gardening offers a versatile, adaptable approach to cultivating plants in harmony. It's about creating a mini-ecosystem where each plant contributes to the health and well-being of its neighbors.

We'll share inspiring stories from real-life gardens, where beginners like you have transformed their spaces into thriving, productive, and beautiful green areas. These tales aren't just anecdotes; they're proof of the magic that happens when you pair the right plants together.

So, let's embark on this green journey together. As you turn each page, imagine your hands in the soil, the sun on your back, and the joy of watching your garden flourish. Welcome to the world of companion gardening – a world where every plant tells a story, and every garden becomes a testament to harmony and collaboration.

What is Companion Planting?

At its core, companion gardening is an age-old, yet ever-evolving practice that intertwines the art of planting different species together to the mutual benefit of each. It's a method steeped in tradition and backed by science, a dance of nature where each plant plays a unique role in supporting its neighbor.

The concept of companion gardening is simple yet profound. It involves strategically placing plants in close proximity so they can provide various benefits to each other. These benefits range from pest control and improved pollination to better use of space and enhanced growth rates. In essence, companion gardening is about creating a diverse, interdependent ecosystem where each plant contributes to the health and success of the whole garden.

Companion gardening goes beyond merely planting different species side by side. It's about understanding the specific needs and characteristics of each plant and how they can complement one another. For example, some plants might repel pests that commonly afflict their neighbors, while others may provide necessary shade or support. It's a harmonious relationship where each plant's strengths help mitigate the weaknesses of others.

The advantages of companion gardening are multi-faceted. By fostering biodiversity, companion gardens are typically more resilient to pests and diseases. This natural form of pest control reduces the need for chemical pesticides, leading to a healthier, more organic garden. Moreover, companion planting can improve soil health, conserve water, and even enhance the flavor and yield of your vegetables and herbs.

Historically, companion gardening has roots in various ancient agricultural practices worldwide. Indigenous cultures have long recognized the wisdom in planting certain crops together, a knowledge that has been passed down through generations. The famous "Three Sisters" method used by Native

American tribes, which combines corn, beans, and squash, is a classic example of companion planting that has endured through time.

In the modern context, companion gardening resonates strongly with urban gardeners and those with limited space. It offers a practical solution for maximizing yield in small areas. Beyond the garden's borders, companion planting is a reflection of a broader movement towards sustainable living and ecological awareness.

As we delve deeper into the specifics of companion gardening, remember that this practice is as much about patience and observation as it is about planting and harvesting. It's a journey that invites you to connect deeply with the natural world, to understand the subtle interactions within your garden, and to become a part of the living tapestry that you create.

Benefits of Companion Planting

Embarking on a journey of companion gardening is similar to nurturing a symphony in nature, where each plant plays a vital role in a harmonious ensemble. This ancient practice, interwoven with ecological wisdom and practicality, offers a plethora of benefits that extend beyond the boundaries of traditional gardening. Let's immerse ourselves in the rich tapestry of advantages that companion gardening unfolds.

Creating a Symphony of Plant Health and Growth: In the realm of companion gardening, plants become more than mere neighbors; they transform into allies, each enhancing the other's vitality. Take, for instance, the marigolds, which, like vigilant guardians, emit substances det

erring harmful nematodes, thus shielding their neighboring plants. Imagine the towering sunflowers, acting as gentle giants providing a canopy of shade to their smaller, sun-sensitive companions below. This natural synergy between plants not only fosters a robust garden but also illustrates the profound interconnectedness in nature.

COMPANION PLANTING FOR BEGINNERS

Harnessing Nature for Pest Control: One of the most significant triumphs of companion gardening is its organic approach to pest management. By thoughtfully pairing plants, such as the aromatic basil and rosemary, gardeners can create a natural shield, deterring pests from more susceptible plants. This strategy weaves a tapestry of balance in the garden ecosystem, reducing the need for chemical interventions and preserving the integrity of the natural world.

Pollination: A Dance of Diversity: In a companion garden, diversity is not just visual; it's functional. The variety of plants attracts a multitude of pollinators, essential for fruit and seed production. Imagine your garden abuzz with bees, fluttering butterflies, and other beneficial insects, each contributing to the flourishing of your garden. This bustling activity not only enhances the garden's productivity but also contributes to the greater ecological narrative.

Spatial Harmony and Efficiency: Companion gardening is particularly adept at maximizing limited spaces. Envision a garden where vertical climbers like beans ascend cornstalks, creating a living trellis. This intelligent use of space exemplifies how understanding the unique growth patterns and needs of different plants can lead to a harmonious and efficient garden layout.

Cultivating Soil Health: The health of the soil is paramount in a companion garden. Plants like legumes play a pivotal role, fixing nitrogen in the soil and enriching it for their neighbors. This practice fosters a sustainable soil ecosystem, reducing reliance on chemical fertilizers and enhancing soil fertility for future growth.

Maximizing Yield Through Mutual Support: In a companion garden, the collective well-being of plants leads to bountiful harvests.

.The cooperative existence among companion plants minimizes competition for resources, allowing each plant to thrive. Gardeners often marvel at how the combined yield of companion-planted crops surpasses that of separately grown plants. This synergy is not just about growing more; it's about growing better, together.

A Tapestry of Aesthetics and Biodiversity: Companion gardens are a visual and ecological delight. Their varied plant life brings a richness of color, texture, and form, creating an aesthetically pleasing landscape. Beyond beauty, these diverse plantings cultivate a mini-ecosystem, inviting beneficial insects and wildlife, thereby contributing to biodiversity conservation. This natural mosaic is a testament to the garden's role as an ecological sanctuary.

Nurturing Personal Satisfaction and Community: The rewards of companion gardening transcend the tangible yields. It's a journey that nurtures a deep connection with nature, offering a serene retreat and a sense of fulfillment. This practice also fosters community spirit, as gardeners share experiences, tips, and the fruits of their labor. It's a process that binds individuals together in a shared love for the earth and its bounty.

Companion gardening is more than a technique; it's a holistic approach that enriches the garden and the gardener alike. As we progress through this guide, these benefits will unfold in practical and relatable ways, showcasing how the art of companion gardening can transform gardens and lives alike, one plant pairing at a time.

Case Studies: Real-Life Success Stories

To truly appreciate the impact of companion gardening, let's explore some real-life success stories. These case studies not only highlight the practical benefits of companion gardening but also showcase the personal journeys of individuals who transformed their gardening spaces into thriving ecosystems.

The Urban Balcony Oasis

Sarah's Story

Living in a high-rise apartment in the city, Sarah thought her dream of gardening was out of reach. With just a small balcony, she started with a few pots of herbs and tomatoes. After learning about companion planting, Sarah strategically added marigolds to deter pests and planted basil alongside her tomatoes, enhancing their growth and flavor. Her balcony transformed into a lush, productive space, becoming a source of pride and a talking point in her urban community.

The Suburban Edible Landscape

The Johnson Family

The Johnsons had a typical suburban lawn, which they converted into an edible landscape through companion gardening. They planted corn, beans, and squash together (the "Three Sisters" method), which significantly improved their yield. The beans fixed nitrogen in the soil, the corn provided a structure for the beans to climb, and the squash leaves shaded the soil, conserving moisture. Their garden became a neighborhood sensation and inspired others to explore sustainable gardening.

The Community Garden Transformation

Green Haven Community Garden

A local community garden was struggling with pest problems and low yield. Volunteers introduced companion planting, intermixing flowers like lavender and nasturtium with vegetables to attract pollinators and deter pests. This not only increased their vegetable yield but also brought a vibrant variety of colors and scents to the garden, fostering a sense of community and connection among the gardeners.

The School Garden Project

Maplewood Elementary School

At Maplewood Elementary, a school garden became a living classroom. Students planted tomatoes, lettuce, and carrots with companions like chives and garlic. This hands-on experience taught children about ecological relationships, plant biology, and the importance of sustainable practices. The garden's success sparked a sense of wonder and respect for nature among the students.

The Rooftop Revolution

Alex's Urban Farm

Alex transformed a neglected rooftop into a flourishing urban farm using companion planting principles. By pairing plants with complementary water and sunlight needs, he maximized the limited space and resources. His rooftop farm not only provided fresh produce but also became a green retreat in the heart of the city.

These stories are a testament to the power of companion gardening to transform spaces, lives, and communities. They illustrate that regardless of where you live or your level of gardening experience, you can create a thriving garden through the principles of companionship and collaboration.

Getting Started with Companion Planting

Embarking on the journey of companion planting is an exciting venture, one that opens up a world of possibilities in even the smallest of spaces. This chapter, "Getting Started with Companion Gardening," is designed to guide you step-by-step through the initial stages of creating your very own companion garden. Whether you have a sprawling backyard, a modest patio, or just a sunny windowsill, this guide will provide the foundational knowledge and confidence you need to begin.

Companion gardening is a practice that's as rewarding as it is enriching. It's not just about growing plants side by side; it's about fostering a symbiotic relationship between them, creating a living, breathing ecosystem right in your backyard or balcony. The beauty of companion gardening lies in its accessibility and adaptability – it can be tailored to suit any space and experience level.

In this chapter, we'll start with the basics, ensuring you have a solid understanding of what you need to begin. We'll cover everything from selecting the right tools and materials to understanding the unique characteristics of your gardening space. This chapter is your roadmap to starting your companion gardening journey, equipped with all the necessary tools and insights.

As you read through, remember that every great garden, no matter its size, starts with a single step. Your companion gardening adventure is about to begin, and the possibilities are as boundless as your imagination. Let's nurture your green thumb and transform your space into a thriving, productive, and harmonious garden.

Essential Tools and Materials

As you embark on your companion gardening journey, having the right tools and materials at hand is crucial for a smooth and enjoyable experience. I will outlines the essentials you'll need to begin cultivating your garden. These tools and materials are the backbone of your gardening activities, helping you work efficiently and effectively.

1. Gardening Tools:

- **Hand Trowel:** An indispensable tool for planting, transplanting, and potting. Look for a sturdy, comfortable trowel that feels good in your hand.

- **Pruning Shears:** Essential for trimming and shaping plants. Opt for a pair that's sharp, durable, and fits comfortably in your hand.

- **Garden Fork and Spade:** These are crucial for turning soil, aerating, and digging. Choose ones with a comfortable grip and robust construction.

- **Watering Can or Hose:** Consistent watering is key. A watering can with a long spout offers precision, while a hose with a spray attachment is ideal for larger gardens.

- **Gloves:** Protect your hands from thorns, splinters, and dirt. Breathable, well-fitted gloves can make a significant difference.

2. Planting Materials:

- **Quality Soil:** Good soil is the foundation of a healthy garden. Consider a mix that's appropriate for the type of plants you're growing.

COMPANION PLANTING FOR BEGINNERS

- **Compost:** This organic matter is gold for gardens, enriching the soil and providing nutrients to your plants.

- **Mulch:** Mulch helps retain soil moisture, suppress weeds, and improve soil quality.

3. Containers and Planters (for Limited Spaces):

- If you're working with a balcony or patio, select containers and planters that fit your space. Ensure they have adequate drainage.

4. Seeds and Seedlings:

- Choose a variety of seeds and seedlings that are suitable for companion planting. Research which plants grow well together for the most successful pairings.

5. Plant Supports:

- For plants that climb or need support, such as tomatoes or beans, consider stakes, trellises, or cages.

6. Labels and Markers:

- Keep track of what you've planted and where with labels or markers. This organization is especially helpful for companion planting.

7. Watering and Fertilizer Schedule:

- Create a schedule to track watering and fertilizing. Consistency is key for plant health, especially in the early stages of growth.

8. Reference Materials:

- Keep a gardening book or guide handy, especially one focused on companion planting, for quick reference and troubleshooting.

Remember, the joy of gardening is as much in the journey as it is in the outcome. While these tools and materials are essential, the most important ingredient is your enthusiasm and willingness to learn. As you gather these items, envision the thriving garden they will help you create – a space where companionship and harmony underpin the beauty and abundance of nature.

Understanding Your Space: From Balconies to Yards

Every gardening space, whether it's a sprawling yard or a compact balcony, holds unique possibilities for companion gardening. This subchapter is dedicated to helping you understand and make the most of the space you have available. It's about seeing potential in every nook and corner and turning it into a thriving garden space.

Assessing Your Space:

Start by assessing the size and characteristics of your gardening area. Measure the dimensions of your space and observe the amount of sunlight it receives throughout the day. Note any existing elements like walls, fences, or large trees that might affect sunlight exposure and wind patterns. Understanding these factors is crucial in deciding what and where to plant.

Sunlight and Shade:

Plants have varying requirements for sunlight. Some thrive in full sun, while others prefer partial shade. Observe the patterns of sunlight in your space and categorize areas as full sun, partial sun, partial shade, or full shade. This will guide you in selecting the right plants for each area of your garden.

Soil Quality:

For ground-level gardens, assess the soil quality. Is it sandy, clayey, or loamy? Does it drain well? You might need to amend the soil with compost or other organic matter to improve its quality. For balcony or patio gardens, selecting high-quality potting mix is key.

Water Access:

Consider the ease of watering your garden. For balconies and patios, a watering can may suffice, but for larger gardens, you might consider hose access or even a drip irrigation system for efficiency and water conservation.

Maximizing Small Spaces:

If you're working with a small space like a balcony or patio, think vertically. Use hanging baskets, wall planters, or trellises to grow upwards. Companion planting in containers can be highly effective, but it's important to consider the root space and watering needs of each plant.

Larger Spaces and Landscaping:

With more space, you have the flexibility to create diverse plant ecosystems. You can dedicate different areas for various companion planting groups. For example, a corner for the 'Three Sisters' (corn, beans, and squash) and another area for herbs and flowers that attract pollinators.

The Importance of Rotation:

In larger gardens, rotating crops yearly in the companion planting setup is beneficial. This practice helps prevent soil depletion and disrupts pest and disease cycles.

Creating a Garden Layout:

Sketch a layout of your garden, keeping in mind the companion planting principles. This plan doesn't have to be perfect; it's a living document that can evolve as your garden grows.

By understanding and respecting the unique characteristics of your space, you can create a harmonious and productive garden. Whether it's the charm of a balcony garden or the expanse of a backyard, your space has the potential to become an ecosystem where plants support and enhance each other's growth.

Initial Planning and Setup for Beginners and Beyond

Embarking on your companion gardening journey requires thoughtful planning and a structured approach, especially for beginners. This subchapter aims to guide you through the initial stages of setting up your companion garden, ensuring a solid foundation for a flourishing and productive space.

Setting Goals and Expectations:

Begin by defining what you want to achieve with your garden. Are you looking to grow fresh herbs and vegetables, create a beautiful floral display, or perhaps a combination of both? Your goals will influence the types of plants you choose and how you organize them.

Researching Plant Companions:

The core of companion gardening lies in understanding which plants benefit each other. Spend time researching compatible plant pairings. Some plants, like tomatoes and basil, not only grow well together but can also enhance each other's flavors. Others, like carrots and onions, work together to repel pests.

Seasonal Planning:

Consider the seasons and climate in your area. This will determine the best time to start planting. Most regions have specific planting windows for different types of plants. Aligning your garden's setup with these windows is crucial for success.

Drawing a Garden Layout:

With your plant pairings in mind, sketch a rough layout of your garden. This doesn't have to be a work of art – a simple diagram showing where each plant will go is sufficient. Remember to consider the height, spread, and growth habits of each plant to avoid overcrowding and ensure adequate sunlight for all.

COMPANION PLANTING FOR BEGINNERS

Soil Preparation:

For ground-level gardens, prepare your soil by removing weeds, loosening it with a garden fork, and enriching it with compost. For container gardens, select high-quality potting soil that will provide the right nutrients and drainage for your plants.

Acquiring Your Plants:

Decide whether you'll start from seeds or seedlings. While seeds can be more cost-effective and offer a wider variety, seedlings can provide a head start, especially useful for beginners or late starters in the gardening season.

Planting Basics:

Follow the guidelines for planting depths and spacing as indicated for your chosen plants. Ensure that companion plants are placed close enough to benefit each other but with enough room to grow without competition.

Watering and Feeding:

Develop a consistent watering schedule. Early morning is typically the best time to water, reducing evaporation and fungal diseases. Learn about the specific feeding needs of your plants – some might require additional fertilization, while others will thrive on compost alone.

Monitoring and Adjusting:

Once your garden is planted, monitor its progress. You may need to make adjustments, such as adding more compost, adjusting watering schedules, or even replanting if a particular pairing doesn't work as expected.

Remember, companion gardening is a learning process filled with trial, error, and adaptation. Each season will bring new insights and opportunities for growth. With patience and persistence, you'll watch your garden transform into a vibrant, interdependent ecosystem that provides joy, produce, and a deep sense of accomplishment.

Comprehensive Companion Plant Guide

Welcome to the heart of companion gardening - the Comprehensive Companion Plant Guide. This chapter is the cornerstone of your gardening journey, where you'll learn the intricacies and wonders of plant relationships. Understanding which plants thrive together and which do not is key to creating a harmonious and productive garden.

In companion gardening, every plant is a character in a larger story, each with its own role and relationships. Like characters in a well-written novel, these plant pairings can support and enhance one another, creating a narrative of growth, health, and mutual benefit. This guide will introduce you to these characters and their dynamic interactions, helping you make informed decisions about which plants to pair in your garden.

We'll delve into detailed lists of common plants, exploring their preferred companions, and the reasons behind these pairings. From the common vegetables in your kitchen to the fragrant herbs and colorful flowers that can adorn your garden, you'll discover a world of combinations and the benefits they bring.

Understanding the interactions between different plants goes beyond just knowing which plants grow well together. It's about understanding the 'why'

- why certain plants repel pests for their neighbors, why some enhance the flavor of others, and why some combinations should be avoided. This knowledge is not only fascinating but also immensely practical, helping you create a garden that is both beautiful and bountiful.

This guide is not just a list; it's a toolkit for smarter gardening. Whether you're a seasoned gardener looking to refine your craft or a beginner starting your first garden, the insights here will be invaluable. We'll cover a range of plants suitable for various environments and preferences, ensuring there's something for every type of gardener.

So, let's turn the page and start exploring the wonderful world of companion plants. Your garden, no matter how big or small, is a canvas awaiting your creativity and care. With this guide, you'll be equipped to paint a vibrant picture of health, harmony, and productivity.

Detailed List of Common Plants and Their Companions

Now, we dive into the heart of companion gardening by exploring a detailed list of common plants and their ideal companions. These pairings are designed to enhance growth, deter pests, and maximize the use of your garden space. Here's a guide to some popular plant companionships, offering you a blueprint for a thriving garden ecosystem.

1. Tomatoes

- •**Companions:** Basil, Marigold, Carrots, Onions, Parsley, and Lettuce.

- •**Benefits:** Basil repels flies and mosquitoes, improves flavor. Marigolds deter nematodes. Carrots and tomatoes grow well together, sharing space without competition.

- •**Avoid:** Planting with cabbage family (broccoli, kale) as they can inhibit each other's growth.

2. Beans

- **Companions:** Corn, Squash, Rosemary, Nasturtium, and Marigolds.

- **Benefits:** Corn provides a natural trellis for beans, and beans fix nitrogen in the soil beneficial for corn. Nasturtium and marigold repel bean beetles.

- **Avoid:** Planting with onions and garlic, as they can stunt the growth of beans.

3. Lettuce

- **Companions:** Carrots, Radish, Strawberries, and Cucumbers.

- **Benefits:** Carrots and radishes help to break up the soil for lettuce roots. Strawberries provide ground cover and reduce weeds.

- **Avoid:** Planting near cabbage family as they can deplete the soil nutrients needed by lettuce.

4. Carrots

- **Companions:** Tomatoes, Onions, Leeks, and Rosemary.

- **Benefits:** Tomatoes release solanine, a natural insecticide, beneficial for carrots. Onions and leeks repel carrot flies.

- **Avoid:** Planting with dill as it can inhibit carrot growth.

5. Cucumbers

- **Companions:** Beans, Peas, Radishes, and Sunflowers.

- **Benefits:** Beans fix nitrogen, helping cucumbers. Sunflowers provide a sturdy support structure.

- **Avoid:** Planting with aromatic herbs or potatoes, which can harm cucumber growth.

6. Peppers

- **Companions:** Basil, Onions, Spinach, and Carrots.

- **Benefits:** Basil repels aphids, spider mites, mosquitoes, and flies. Onions deter pests and disease.

- **Avoid:** Planting with beans and kohlrabi, which can impede pepper growth.

7. Squash

- **Companions:** Corn, Beans, Nasturtiums, and Marigolds.

- **Benefits:** The "Three Sisters" method with corn and beans is ideal. Nasturtiums and marigolds repel squash bugs and beetles.

- **Avoid:** Planting with potatoes, as they can compete for nutrients.

8. Herbs

- **General Companions:** Most vegetables benefit from being planted near herbs due to their natural pest-repelling properties.

- **Specific Pairings:** Rosemary with beans, basil with tomatoes, chives with carrots.

- **Note:** Some herbs like mint can be invasive and are best grown in containers.

This list is a starting point, offering a glimpse into the diverse world of companion planting. As you experiment with these and other combinations, observe how they interact in your unique garden environment. Companion planting is as much an art as it is a science, one that evolves with experience and adaptation.

Tailored Recommendations for Urban Gardens

Urban gardening presents unique challenges and opportunities, especially when it comes to companion planting. Limited space, varying light conditions, and the urban microclimate all play a role in shaping your garden. This subchapter offers tailored recommendations for urban gardens, helping you make the most of your space through thoughtful companion planting.

1. Maximizing Limited Space:

- •**Vertical Planting:** Utilize vertical space with trellises, wall planters, or hanging baskets. Plants like beans, peas, and some varieties of squash and cucumbers can climb, saving ground space for other crops.

- •**Container Combinations:** Pair plants in containers based on their size and needs. For example, shallow-rooted herbs like basil can grow in the same pot with deeper-rooted plants like tomatoes.

2. Balancing Light and Shade:

- •**Sun-Loving Pairs:** In areas that receive ample sunlight, combine sun-loving plants like tomatoes with basil or peppers with marigolds.

- •**Shade-Tolerant Combinations:** For shaded areas, pair leafy greens like lettuce or spinach with herbs that can tolerate less sun, such as parsley or cilantro.

3. Dealing with Pests and Pollution:

- •**Natural Pest Deterrents:** In urban areas, pests can be a significant challenge. Utilize plants like lavender, chives, and marigolds, which naturally repel common pests.

- •**Pollution-Tolerant Plants:** Some plants are more resilient to urban pollution. Consider hardier plants like kale, chard, and certain herbs for areas with higher exposure to urban elements.

4. Edible and Aesthetic Balance:

- •**Decorative and Productive:** Urban gardens often serve both aesthetic and functional purposes. Integrate ornamental plants that have companion benefits, such as nasturtiums (edible and beneficial for many vegetables) or flowering herbs like chives.

5. Utilizing Window Boxes and Balconies:

- •**Herb and Salad Boxes:** Grow a mix of herbs like thyme, oregano, and mint alongside leafy greens in window boxes. They're easy to access for kitchen use and can thrive in smaller spaces.

- •**Balcony Rail Planters:** Utilize rail planters for shallow-rooted plants and herbs, or for flowers that attract pollinators to support other plants in your garden.

6. Water Management:

- •**Conserving Water:** In urban settings, efficient water use is crucial. Implement drip irrigation or self-watering planters to conserve water and ensure consistent moisture.

7. Community and Shared Spaces:

- •**Community Gardening:** If you have access to a community garden, engage in shared companion planting projects. This not only maximizes space but also fosters community learning and support.

Urban gardening, with its constraints, also offers a canvas for creativity and innovation. Through companion planting, you can create a vibrant, productive, and sustainable garden in the heart of the city. These tailored recommendations are designed to help you navigate the unique aspects of urban gardening, turning challenges into opportunities for a thriving green space.

Seasonal and Climate Considerations

Understanding the seasonal and climate considerations is vital in companion gardening. This subchapter is dedicated to helping you navigate these factors, ensuring your garden thrives in sync with the natural rhythms of your environment. Whether you're dealing with a harsh winter, a scorching summer, or a temperate climate, adapting your companion gardening strategy accordingly can make all the difference.

1. Understanding Your Climate Zone:

Understanding your climate zone is a fundamental step in tailoring your garden to its environment, ensuring the plants you choose are well-suited to thrive in your specific conditions. It's about aligning your gardening efforts with the rhythms of your local ecosystem, which ultimately leads to a more successful and sustainable garden.

What is a Climate Zone? A climate zone is a defined area that shares similar average temperatures and weather patterns throughout the year. These zones are crucial in determining which plants are best suited to grow in a particular region. They guide gardeners on what to plant, when to plant it, and how to care for it, considering the unique environmental conditions of each area.

Identifying Your Climate Zone:

- •**Use of Tools like the USDA Plant Hardiness Zone Map:** This map divides North America into zones based on the average annual minimum winter temperature. By finding your location on this map, you can determine your specific zone.

- •**Interpreting the Map:** Each zone on the map has a unique climate profile that influences the types of plants that can grow there and their optimal growing seasons. For example, a plant that thrives in the warm, year-round growing season of zone 10 might struggle in the cooler, shorter growing season of zone 5.

COMPANION PLANTING FOR BEGINNERS

Why Climate Zones Matter:

- **Plant Survival and Health:** Plants vary in their temperature tolerance. Knowing your climate zone helps you select plants that can survive and thrive in your local weather conditions.

- **Seasonal Planning:** Different zones have different frost dates and length of growing seasons. Understanding your zone allows for more accurate planning of planting and harvesting times. For instance, gardeners in cooler zones need to be aware of the last frost date in spring to avoid planting tender plants too early.

Applying Climate Zone Knowledge:

- **Tailored Plant Selection:** Choose plants that are recommended for your zone. This increases the chances of plant survival and reduces the need for excessive care and protection from unsuitable weather conditions.

- **Gardening Strategies:** Your gardening strategies, such as mulching for winter protection or providing shade during the hottest months, will be influenced by the specific needs of your climate zone. For instance, in a cooler climate zone, you might focus on maximizing sunlight exposure and protecting plants from frost, while in a warmer zone, your priority might be ensuring adequate hydration and shading to protect plants from excessive heat.

- **Adaptation to Changes:** Even within your climate zone, microclimates, such as those created by urban areas or bodies of water, can affect your garden. Being aware of these nuances helps in fine-tuning your gardening approach to match local conditions.

- **Future Planning:** With climate patterns evolving, keeping an eye on how your zone might be changing over the years is important. This foresight can help you adapt your garden to shifting conditions, such as choosing drought-resistant varieties in areas becoming warmer and drier.

Understanding your climate zone is like having a roadmap for your garden. It guides your decisions and helps you create a garden that is in harmony with its natural surroundings. This knowledge, coupled with local observations and adaptations, lays the foundation for a resilient and fruitful gardening experience.

2. Seasonal Plant Selection:

Seasonal plant selection in companion gardening is about understanding and leveraging the natural ebb and flow of the seasons. Each season brings its own set of optimal growing conditions, and selecting plants that thrive in these conditions can significantly enhance the health and yield of your garden. Let's delve deeper into the seasonal rhythms and how to align your gardening practices with them.

Spring Planting: Spring is characterized by milder temperatures and the awakening of the garden. This season is ideal for cool-season crops that can tolerate the cooler temperatures and even a light frost.

- **Examples of Spring Crops:** Lettuce, peas, and spinach are classic cool-weather crops. They germinate and grow well in the cooler temperatures of spring and can be harvested before the summer heat sets in.

- **Companion Planting in Spring:** Companion planting these vegetables with herbs like cilantro, which also prefer cooler temperatures, can be beneficial. For example, cilantro may help repel pests from your lettuce, providing a natural form of pest control.

Summer Gardening: As the temperatures rise, the garden shifts to warm-season crops that love the heat and sun.

- **Examples of Summer Crops:** Tomatoes, peppers, and cucumbers thrive in the warmth of summer. They need longer daylight hours and warmer temperatures to grow and produce fruit.

- **Companion Planting in Summer:** Basil and marigolds are excellent companions for these summer crops. Basil is known to improve the flavor of tomatoes and repel harmful pests like mosquitoes and flies. Marigolds are particularly useful for repelling nematodes in the soil, which can negatively affect tomato plants.

Fall Harvest: Fall brings cooler temperatures, making it suitable for a second round of cool-season crops.

- •**Examples of Fall Crops:** This is a great time to plant kale, carrots, and beets. These crops can tolerate the cooler weather and mature in conditions that would be too harsh for summer crops.

- •**Companion Planting in Fall:** Planting garlic near roses or raspberries can enhance their growth and health. Garlic acts as a natural repellent for several pests and can prevent fungal diseases.

Winter Considerations: In milder climates, winter doesn't mean the end of gardening.

- •**Winter Crops:** Hardy greens like collards and Swiss chard can still be grown. These plants can survive cold temperatures and even improve in flavor after a frost.

- •**Gardening in Colder Areas:** In areas with harsh winters, this season is more about preparation and planning for spring.

It's a time to reflect on the past year's successes and challenges and to plan for the upcoming growing seasons. Gardeners might spend this time poring over seed catalogs, designing next year's garden layout, or preparing indoor seed starting setups for early spring plantings.

Integrating Seasonal Knowledge into Gardening:

- •**Understanding Seasonal Growth Cycles:** Different plants have adapted to grow best in certain seasonal conditions. By aligning your planting schedule with these natural cycles, you can maximize growth and yield.

- •**Transitioning Between Seasons:** As one season transitions to the next, it's important to adjust your gardening practices. This might include changing the types of crops you plant, modifying your watering schedule, or altering your pest management strategies.

- **Utilizing Succession Planting:** To maintain a continuous harvest, consider succession planting. For example, as early spring crops like lettuce are harvested, space can be used for late spring plantings of heat-loving crops.

Seasonal Companion Planting:

- **Leveraging Companion Benefits:** Different companion plants offer various benefits throughout the seasons, from pest control to soil improvement. By selecting companions that are beneficial for the current season's crops, you can create a more harmonious and productive garden.

- **Adapting to Seasonal Pests and Diseases:** Different pests and diseases are prevalent in different seasons. Using companion plants that repel or resist these seasonal challenges can help keep your garden healthy year-round.

Seasonal plant selection in companion gardening is about more than just choosing plants that will survive; it's about selecting plants that will thrive in the current season's conditions. By understanding and embracing the rhythms of the seasons, and by thoughtfully pairing plants that complement and support each other during these times, you can create a garden that is not only productive but also in tune with the natural world.

3. Adapting to Weather Extremes:

Adapting to weather extremes in companion gardening involves implementing strategies to protect and support your plants during periods of unusual weather conditions, such as heatwaves or cold snaps. These extremes can stress plants and disrupt the delicate balance of your garden ecosystem. Let's explore how to effectively navigate these challenges.

Adapting to Heatwaves: Heatwaves bring intense heat and sunlight, which can be stressful for many plants, especially those that are not heat-tolerant.

•**Adequate Watering:** During heatwaves, the soil can dry out rapidly. Ensuring that your plants receive adequate water is crucial. This may mean increasing the frequency or quantity of watering. However, it's important to water deeply and less frequently rather than shallow and often, to encourage deep root growth which helps plants access moisture from deeper in the soil.

•**Use of Shade Cloth:** Shade cloth can be a gardener's best friend during a heatwave. It provides a barrier between the sun and the plants, reducing the intensity of the sunlight and helping to lower the temperature around the plants. This is particularly helpful for young, tender plants or those that prefer cooler conditions.

•**Grouping Plants by Water Needs:** Companion planting can play a role in managing water use during a heatwave. By grouping plants with similar water requirements together, you can water more efficiently. For example, grouping moisture-loving plants together allows you to concentrate watering in specific areas, ensuring that these plants receive the moisture they need without overwatering more drought-tolerant plants.

Managing Frost and Cold Snaps: Unexpected cold weather can be just as challenging as heatwaves, particularly for plants that are sensitive to frost.

•**Using Cold Frames and Row Covers:** Cold frames and row covers are effective tools for protecting plants from frost. They act as a physical barrier, trapping heat around the plants and shielding them from the cold. Cold frames are particularly useful for extending the growing season of cool-weather crops like leafy greens, allowing them to continue growing even as temperatures drop.

•**Choosing Hardy Companion Plants:** Some plants are more tolerant of cold than others. Planting hardy companions, such as onions, near more sensitive plants can offer some degree of protection. The hardier plants can act as a windbreak or provide some shelter, creating a slightly warmer microclimate. This can be particularly beneficial for plants that are on the edge of their tolerance for cold weather.

- •**Strategic Plant Placement:** Positioning sensitive plants in areas of your garden that are less exposed to cold winds and frost can also help. For example, planting near a south-facing wall can provide extra warmth and protection.

- •**Utilizing Thermal Mass:** Objects like stones, bricks, or water containers can absorb heat during the day and release it slowly at night, creating a warmer microclimate. Strategically placing these objects near sensitive plants can help mitigate the effects of sudden temperature drops.

Overall, adapting to weather extremes in companion gardening is about being proactive and responsive to the needs of your plants under challenging conditions. It involves a combination of practical strategies, such as watering and providing physical protection, and thoughtful garden planning, such as grouping plants with similar needs and using the garden's microclimate to your advantage. By taking these steps, you can help ensure that your garden remains healthy and productive, even when the weather is not ideal.

4. Soil Considerations:

Soil is often considered the foundation of a successful garden, and its health and composition are significantly influenced by the climate. Understanding how different climatic conditions affect soil is crucial in companion gardening, as it enables you to tailor your soil management practices to ensure optimal plant growth and health.

Impact of Climate on Soil Conditions:

1.Rainy Climates and Nutrient Leaching:

- •In areas with high rainfall, the soil can face the issue of nutrient leaching. This occurs when excess water washes away essential nutrients, such as nitrogen, potassium, and phosphorus, making them less available to plants.

- Heavy rains can also lead to soil erosion, stripping away the top fertile layer of the soil. This can reduce the soil's organic matter content and its ability to retain moisture and nutrients.

- Solution: To combat nutrient leaching, consider incorporating organic matter like compost or well-rotted manure into the soil. These materials can improve soil structure, enhance nutrient retention, and stimulate microbial activity, thereby replenishing and maintaining nutrient levels. Additionally, using mulch can help reduce surface runoff and protect the soil from erosion.

2.Dry Climates and Soil Compaction:

- In dryer climates, the lack of moisture can lead to soil compaction, where the soil particles are pressed tightly together, reducing pore space. This makes it difficult for roots to penetrate and can impede water infiltration and aeration.

- Compacted soil often has poor drainage and can become hard and crusty, further challenging plant growth.

- Solution: Regularly amending the soil with organic matter can help improve its structure and water-holding capacity. Organic matter acts as a soil conditioner, breaking up compacted soil and increasing its ability to hold water and nutrients. In extreme cases, employing techniques like aeration, where small holes are made in the soil to allow air, water, and nutrients to penetrate, can be beneficial.

3.Utilizing Raised Beds:

- In both rainy and dry climates, raised beds offer an effective solution for managing soil conditions. By elevating the soil above ground level, raised beds provide better drainage in wet areas and improved soil conditions in dry areas.

- Raised beds allow for better control over the soil's composition and moisture levels. You can fill them with a balanced mix of soil, compost, and other organic materials to create an optimal growing environment for your plants.

4.Monitoring and Adjusting pH Levels:

- Soil pH, which measures how acidic or alkaline your soil is, can also be influenced by your climate. For instance, rainfall can gradually acidify soil over time.

- Regularly testing your soil's pH and adjusting it as needed is an important part of soil management. You can use lime to raise the pH of overlyacidic soil or sulfur to lower the pH of alkaline soil. The goal is to maintain a pH level that is conducive to the plants you are growing, as pH affects nutrient availability to plants.

5.Mulching for Temperature and Moisture Control:

- Mulching is another crucial aspect of soil management, particularly in extreme climates. In hot, dry climates, mulch helps retain soil moisture and keeps the soil cooler. In wet climates, it can prevent soil erosion and protect against nutrient leaching.

- Organic mulches, such as straw, bark, or leaf mold, not only moderate soil temperature and moisture but also gradually break down and add organic matter to the soil, enhancing its fertility and structure over time.

Customizing Soil Management Practices:

- **Personal Observation and Adaptation:** It's important to observe how your specific garden soil responds to the local climate and adjust your practices accordingly. For instance, if you notice water pooling on the soil surface during heavy rains, improving drainage becomes a priority.

- **Adapting to Seasonal Changes:** Soil management is not a one-time task but an ongoing process. The strategies might vary with seasonal changes. For instance, you might need to increase organic matter addition during the wet season to counteract leaching or increase mulching in summer to conserve moisture.

- **Companion Planting Considerations:** When planning your companion planting, consider how different plants can support soil health. For example, planting nitrogen-fixing legumes can benefit neighboring plants in nutrient-depleted soils.

Understanding and adapting to the ways in which climate affects soil conditions is a key component of successful gardening. By being proactive in your soil management practices, you can create a fertile and resilient foundation for your plants to thrive, regardless of the climatic challenges you may face.

5. Water Management:

Effective water management is a pivotal aspect of gardening, particularly in companion planting where the needs of various plants must be harmonized. The way you manage water in your garden greatly depends on the climatic conditions and seasonal changes of your region. Understanding these factors and implementing appropriate watering strategies can significantly enhance the health and productivity of your garden.

Seasonal and Climatic Considerations in Water Management:

1. **Understanding Seasonal Water Needs:**

   - Different seasons bring different water requirements. For instance, the increasing heat and longer daylight hours in summer typically necessitate more frequent watering compared to the cooler, shorter days of autumn.

   - The type of crops grown in each season also influences water needs. Summer crops like tomatoes and cucumbers generally require more water, especially during fruiting, compared to cooler season crops.

2.Watering Practices in Dry Areas:

- In arid or dry climates, water conservation becomes essential. Drip irrigation is an excellent method for such conditions. It delivers water directly to the roots of the plants, minimizing evaporation and ensuring that water is used efficiently.

- Drip systems can be automated and adjusted according to the specific needs of your plants, ensuring that each plant receives the right amount of water without wastage.

- Mulching around your plants is another effective technique in dry areas. It helps retain soil moisture, reduces water evaporation, and keeps the soil temperature regulated.

3.Managing Water in Wet Climates:

- In regions with abundant rainfall, the challenge often lies in preventing excess moisture from harming plants. Good drainage is key to avoid waterlogging, which can lead to root rot and other fungal diseases.

- Raised garden beds can be particularly beneficial in wetter climates as they provide better drainage. Ensuring that your soil has enough organic matter can also improve its structure and drainage capabilities.

- In these climates, it's crucial to monitor rainfall patterns and adjust manual watering accordingly to avoid overwatering.

4.Adjusting Watering Based on Plant Needs:

- Companion planting often involves grouping plants with similar water requirements together. This practice not only simplifies watering routines but also ensures that each plant's water needs are met without overwatering others.

- For example, grouping thirsty plants like lettuce and celery together allows for targeted watering, while drought-tolerant plants like lavender and rosemary can be grouped else-where.

5.Monitoring and Adaptation:

- •Regularly check the moisture level of your soil. This can be as simple as feeling the soil a few inches below the surface. If it's dry, it's time to water; if it's still moist, you can wait.

- •Be adaptive in your approach. Weather patterns can change, and so can the water needs of your garden. Be prepared to adjust your watering practices in response to these changes.

Effective water management in companion gardening requires a thoughtful balance between the climatic conditions, the specific needs of the plants, and the seasonal variations. By tailoring your watering practices to these factors, you can ensure that your garden remains healthy, conserves water, and provides a bountiful harvest.

6. Beneficial Mulching:

Mulching is a multifaceted practice in gardening that provides numerous benefits, making it an essential element in maintaining a healthy and productive garden. The use of mulch, which involves covering the soil with a layer of material, can greatly enhance your garden's environment by conserving moisture, suppressing weeds, protecting plant roots, and enriching the soil. Let's explore the various advantages of mulching and how it can be beneficial throughout the year.

1. Moisture Conservation:

- •In the summer, mulch acts as an insulating layer for the soil, reducing the rate of water evaporation from the soil surface. This is particularly crucial during hot, dry periods when water conservation is essential.

- •By maintaining a more consistent soil moisture level, mulch helps ensure that plants have steady access to the water they need, promoting healthier growth and reducing the stress on plants caused by fluctuating water availability.

2. Weed Suppression:

- Mulch serves as a physical barrier, limiting the amount of sunlight that can reach weed seeds in the soil, thus preventing their germination and growth. This natural weed control method reduces the need for manual weeding and herbicides.

- A thick layer of mulch can effectively smother existing small weeds, preventing them from receiving the light they need to grow, thereby keeping your garden beds cleaner and reducing competition for nutrients and water.

3. Root Protection:

- During winter, mulch acts as an insulating blanket for the soil and plant roots. It helps to moderate the soil temperature, protecting roots from extreme cold and temperature fluctuations that can be harmful to plants.

- This protection is especially important for perennials and newly planted trees and shrubs, helping them to survive the winter and thrive in the following growing season.

4. Soil Enrichment:

- As organic mulches decompose, they add valuable organic matter to the soil, improving its structure, nutrient content, and overall fertility.

- This gradual enrichment of the soil promotes the activity of beneficial soil organisms like earthworms and microbes, which further enhance soil health and structure.

5. Types of Mulch and Application:

- Common organic mulches include straw, bark chips, shredded leaves, and compost. Each type has its benefits and can be selected based on specific garden needs.

- When applying mulch, leave a small space around the base of each plant to prevent potential rot and fungal diseases. The ideal thickness of the mulch layer can vary, but a general guideline is 2-4 inches.

6. Aesthetic Appeal:

- Besides its practical benefits, mulch can also improve the visual appeal of your garden. It provides a uniform, finished look to garden beds and can highlight the plants it surrounds.

Mulching is a simple yet highly effective gardening practice that offers a multitude of benefits across seasons. By incorporating mulching into your gardening routine, you not only enhance the health and productivity of your garden but also contribute to a more sustainable gardening practice. Mulch helps create a more self-sustaining environment where plants can thrive with less intervention, making it a cornerstone of an efficient and eco-friendly garden. Whether you are dealing with the heat of summer or preparing for the chill of winter, mulch is an invaluable ally in the garden, working quietly yet powerfully to ensure the well-being of your plants and the soil they grow in.

7. Pest and Disease Management:

Pest and disease management is a critical aspect of maintaining a healthy and productive garden. Seasonal changes often influence the types of pests and diseases that can affect your plants, and a proactive approach is necessary to mitigate these challenges. Companion planting plays a key role in this strategy by using certain plants' natural properties to repel pests or deter diseases, thus reducing the need for chemical interventions. Let's explore this concept in more depth.

Understanding Seasonal Pest and Disease Dynamics:

COMPANION PLANTING FOR BEGINNERS

- **Spring and Early Summer:** These seasons often see a surge in pest activity as temperatures rise and plants begin new growth. Common pests like aphids, slugs, and caterpillars emerge, seeking out tender new foliage.

- **Late Summer and Fall:** As plants mature, different pests and diseases can become prevalent. These might include mites, beetles, and fungal diseases that thrive in the warmer, sometimes more humid, conditions of late summer.

- **Winter:** While pest activity generally decreases in colder weather, some pests and diseases can overwinter in the soil or on plant debris, ready to re-emerge in spring.

Companion Planting for Pest and Disease Control:

- **Natural Repellents:** Many plants have natural pest-repellent properties. For instance, chives and garlic emit strong scents that deter aphids, making them excellent companions for roses and other aphid-prone plants.

- **Disease Prevention:** Certain companion plants can help prevent diseases. For example, marigolds are known to suppress nematodes in the soil, which can affect a variety of plants.

- **Attracting Beneficial Insects:** Companion plants can also attract beneficial insects that are natural predators of common pests. Plants like dill and fennel attract ladybugs, which feed on aphids.

Integrated Pest Management (IPM):

- **Monitoring:** Regularly inspect your plants for signs of pests or disease. Early detection is key to effective management.

- **Physical Controls:** Techniques like hand-picking pests, using water sprays to dislodge aphids, or applying row covers to protect plants can be effective.

- **Biological Controls:** Introduce or encourage beneficial insects and organisms that naturally control pest populations.

Cultural Practices for Disease Prevention:

- **Good Hygiene:** Remove and dispose of diseased plant material to prevent the spread of pathogens.

- **Proper Spacing:** Ensure plants are not overcrowded, as poor air circulation can promote the development of fungal diseases.

- **Soil Health:** Healthy soil supports strong plant growth, which is more resistant to pests and diseases. Incorporating organic matter and ensuring adequate drainage are key.

Adapting Strategies to Specific Pests and Diseases:

- **Tailored Approaches:** Different pests and diseases require different strategies. For instance,

fungus gnats may be controlled by reducing watering frequency, while aphids might be managed with insecticidal soap or natural predators.

- **Plant-Specific Considerations:** Some plants are more susceptible to certain pests and diseases. Understanding these vulnerabilities can help you tailor your pest and disease management strategies. For example, tomatoes are often prone to blight, so practices like crop rotation and avoiding overhead watering can be beneficial.

Seasonal Adjustments:

- **Spring Preparations:** Early spring is a good time to clean up garden debris, which can harbor pests and diseases. Applying mulch can also help suppress early weed growth, which can attract pests.

- **Summer Vigilance:** Regularly check your plants for signs of infestation or illness, especially during the peak growth period of summer. Adjust watering and feeding as needed to keep plants robust and less susceptible to problems.

- **Fall Cleanup:** Removing spent plants and fallen leaves can reduce over-wintering pest populations and disease spores. This is also a good time to apply compost or other organic matter to improve soil health for the next growing season.

Holistic Approach: Effective pest and disease management in companion gardening is not just about reacting to problems as they arise; it's about creating a healthy, balanced garden ecosystem where problems are less likely to take hold. This involves a combination of proactive strategies, regular monitoring, and adjustments based on the specific needs and conditions of your garden.

By staying vigilant and utilizing companion plants effectively, along with other integrated pest management practices, you can significantly reduce the impact of pests and diseases on your garden. This approach not only protects your plants but also contributes to a more sustainable and environmentally friendly gardening practice.

8. Seasonal Garden Planning:

Seasonal garden planning is a thoughtful process that involves adapting your garden's layout and plant selections to align with the changing seasons. This approach is particularly effective in companion gardening, where understanding the temporal dynamics of plant growth and interactions can significantly enhance the health and productivity of your garden. Let's delve deeper into how seasonal planning and crop rotation can be effectively implemented in your garden.

Understanding Seasonal Garden Dynamics:

- **Spring Planning:** This is a time for planting cool-season crops and early starters. Plan for crops like peas, lettuce, and spinach, which can tolerate cooler temperatures. It's also an ideal time to start many warm-season crops indoors or in a greenhouse for transplanting later.

- **Summer Adaptations:** As temperatures rise, transition to warm-season crops like tomatoes, peppers, and cucumbers. This is also the time to plan for late-summer and fall plantings, ensuring a continuous harvest.

- **Fall Preparations:** In many climates, fall is suitable for planting a second round of cool-season crops and for establishing perennials and trees. The cooler temperatures and increased rainfall can be advantageous for these plants.

- **Winter Strategy:** In colder climates, winter is mostly a time for planning. In milder climates, however, it can be an opportunity to grow hardy crops and to prepare the soil for spring.

Crop Rotation and Companion Planting:

- **Rotating Crops:** Rotating crops annually helps prevent the buildup of pests and diseases in the soil. For example, avoid planting tomatoes or other nightshades in the same spot where they or their relatives grew the previous year.

- **Refreshing Companion Plantings:** Change companion plantings each year to prevent pests and diseases that might have become established from affecting the new crops. This also helps in balancing the nutrient demands on the soil.

- **Soil Enrichment:** Some companion plants, like legumes, enrich the soil by fixing nitrogen, making them excellent choices to precede or follow nutrient-hungry plants like corn or tomatoes.

Planning for Soil Health:

- **Cover Crops:** Incorporate cover crops into your garden rotation, especially during the off-season. Cover crops can improve soil structure, add organic matter, and prevent erosion.

- **Organic Amendments:** Each season, assess and amend the soil with compost, manure, or other organic matter to maintain its fertility and structure.

COMPANION PLANTING FOR BEGINNERS

Tailoring Garden Layout to Seasons:

- **Sunlight and Shade:** Consider the changing patterns of sunlight and shade throughout the seasons and plan your garden layout accordingly. Some plants may benefit from the higher summer sun, while others may need protection from intense heat.

- **Water Requirements:** Plan your garden layout considering the varying water needs of your plants in different seasons. Grouping plants with similar watering needs can make irrigation more efficient.

Planning for Succession Planting:

- **Continuous Harvest:** Utilize succession planting to have a continuous supply of vegetables. As soon as one crop is harvested, have another ready to take its place. This maximizes the productivity of your garden space throughout the growing season.

Seasonal garden planning in companion gardening is about more than just deciding what to plant; it's about creating a dynamic and responsive garden that evolves with the seasons. By thoughtfully rotating crops, adjusting companion plantings, and considering the specific needs of your soil and plants through the seasons, you can create a garden that is not only productive but also sustainable and harmonious with the natural environment. This approach leads to a healthier garden ecosystem, enriched soil, and a bountiful harvest, while also mitigating common gardening challenges such as pest infestations and plant diseases. By embracing the rhythm of the seasons and planning your garden accordingly, you can enjoy the rewards of a flourishing garden that resonates with the cycles of nature.

Designing Your Companion Garden

Embarking on the design phase of your companion garden is where creativity meets functionality. In this chapter we focus on turning your space, whether a sprawling backyard or a cozy balcony, into an aesthetically pleasing yet highly productive area. This journey of design is not just about planting; it's about crafting a living tapestry that is as beautiful as it is beneficial.

The art of garden design in companion planting goes beyond mere aesthetics; it's a thoughtful process of understanding how different plants interact with each other and their environment. It's about creating a harmonious space where each plant contributes to the overall health and beauty of the garden.

We will explore various design elements that are key to companion gardening. From the layout of your garden beds to the choice of color and texture, every decision plays a part in creating a thriving ecosystem. You'll learn how to make the most of your available space, how to arrange plants for optimal growth and health, and how to create a garden that is a joy to behold and a pleasure to tend.

In this chapter, we'll cover:

- **Creative Layouts for Various Spaces:** Tailoring your garden design to fit the shape and size of your available space, utilizing principles that maximize both beauty and productivity.

- **Aesthetic and Functional Container Gardening:** Design tips for those with limited space, focusing on how to arrange containers for both visual appeal and plant health.

- **Vertical Gardening Techniques:** Innovative ways to grow upwards, making the most of vertical spaces for both function and form.

Designing your companion garden is a journey that allows you to express your creativity while adhering to the principles of companion planting. It's about finding balance and harmony, not just for your plants, but also for yourself as a gardener. As we delve into these design principles, you'll be equipped to create a space that reflects your personal style and meets the needs of your plants.

Creative Layouts for Various Spaces

Designing a companion garden is an exercise in creativity, especially when working with diverse spaces. In this subchapter, we'll explore creative layouts that make the most of different types of spaces, from expansive yards to compact urban balconies. These layouts are designed to maximize plant health and productivity, while also creating visually appealing and enjoyable spaces.

1. Small-Space and Urban Layouts:

- **Tiered Planters:** Utilize tiered planters or stepped shelves to grow multiple plants in a compact area. This arrangement allows for ample sunlight exposure for each plant.

- **Hanging Baskets and Window Boxes:** Ideal for herbs and trailing plants like strawberries. They add vertical interest and save valuable floor space.

- **Container Groupings:** Group pots and containers of various sizes together, pairing plants based on their companion benefits. This approach creates a mini ecosystem in each group.

2. Medium-Sized Garden Layouts:

- **Raised Beds:** Ideal for controlling soil quality and drainage. Arrange raised beds in a grid pattern, dedicating each bed to compatible companion plants.

- **Keyhole Gardens:** This design maximizes space and accessibility. A central composting basket nourishes the surrounding plants, making it both functional and sustainable.

- **Border Planting:** Utilize the edges of your space for plants that can repel pests or attract pollinators, creating a natural defense and support system for the rest of the garden.

3. Large Garden Layouts:

- **Companion Planting Blocks:** Segment your garden into blocks, each with its own set of companion plants. This method simplifies crop rotation and pest management.

- **Intercropping Rows:** Plant rows of taller crops like corn or sunflowers, with lower-growing plants beneath. This layout optimizes space and creates a dynamic visual effect.

- **Garden Rooms:** Divide your garden into 'rooms' or sections, each with a different theme or companion grouping. This approach can create a diverse and immersive garden experience.

4. Specialty Layouts:

- **Pollinator-Friendly Garden:** Dedicate a section of your garden to flowering plants that attract pollinators. This not only supports your vegetable crops but also promotes biodiversity.

- **Herb Spiral:** A spiral-shaped garden bed ideal for growing a variety of herbs in a limited space. It provides different microclimates due to variations in soil depth and moisture.

5. Aesthetic Considerations:

- •Consider the visual aspects like color, texture, and height when planning your layout. A mix of flowering plants with vegetables and herbs can create a visually stunning and productive garden.

- •Pathways and borders, whether made from stone, wood chips, or grass, add structure and beauty to the garden.

Remember, the layout of your companion garden should reflect your personal style and the practical needs of your plants. These creative layouts are starting points, inspiring you to experiment and find the best configuration for your space and gardening goals.

Aesthetic and Functional Container Gardening

Container gardening is a versatile and practical solution for those with limited space or challenging soil conditions. In this subchapter, we focus on creating container gardens that are not only functional in terms of plant health and productivity but also aesthetically pleasing. By combining the principles of companion planting with thoughtful design, you can turn containers into vibrant, flourishing parts of your living space.

Choosing the Right Containers:

- •**Size and Material:** Select containers that provide enough space for the roots of your plants to grow. Materials can range from traditional clay and terracotta to modern plastics and recycled materials. Each material has its benefits and aesthetic appeal.

- •**Drainage:** Ensure each container has adequate drainage to prevent waterlogging. You can add holes to containers if needed.

Complementary Plant Pairings:

- •**Visual and Functional Harmony:** Pair plants that not only grow well together but also look good together. For example, a tall, leafy green like kale paired with the bright, sprawling flowers of nasturtiums creates both a visually appealing and beneficial pairing.

- **Root Compatibility:** Consider the root space each plant needs. Shallow-rooted herbs can be planted with deeper-rooted vegetables in larger containers.

Soil and Nutrition:

- **Quality Potting Mix:** Use a high-quality potting mix suited for container gardening. It should be well-draining yet able to retain enough moisture.

- **Nutrient Management:** Regularly check and manage the nutrient levels in your containers, as they can deplete faster than in-ground soil. Compost and organic fertilizers can be added as needed.

Watering Considerations:

- **Consistent Moisture:** Containers can dry out quickly, especially in hot weather. Implement a consistent watering schedule and consider self-watering containers to maintain moisture levels.

- **Mulching:** Use mulch on top of the soil in containers to help retain moisture and reduce water evaporation.

Design and Layout:

- **Grouping Containers:** Arrange containers in groups to create a more cohesive and impactful display. Consider varying the height and size of containers for a dynamic look.

- **Color Coordination:** Coordinate the colors of your containers with the plants and your surrounding decor. This adds an extra layer of visual harmony to your space.

- **Mobile Gardening:** Use stands with wheels for heavier containers to easily move them around for optimal sunlight exposure or aesthetic rearrangement.

Seasonal Adjustments:

- •Change up the plantings in containers with the seasons. This not only keeps your display interesting but also allows you to grow a variety of plants throughout the year.

Container gardening, when done thoughtfully, can transform balconies, patios, and even windowsills into lush, productive gardens. With these tips, your container garden will be a harmonious blend of functionality and beauty, proving that even the smallest spaces can yield abundant and visually stunning results.

Vertical Gardening Techniques

Vertical gardening is a transformative and innovative approach to gardening that opens up a world of possibilities, especially for those with limited space. This method of gardening allows you to elevate your plants, bringing an exciting vertical dimension to the landscape. Whether you have just a small balcony, a modest patio, or even an indoor area, vertical gardening techniques not only maximize your growing space but also add a unique aesthetic appeal to your garden. In this subchapter, we delve into various vertical gardening techniques that are practical, visually stunning, and conducive to growing a diverse range of plants.

Exploring the Heights with Trellises and Climbing Supports: Imagine a garden where plants reach upwards, entwining themselves around trellises and climbing supports. These structures are perfect for plants like beans, peas, cucumbers, certain types of squash, and climbing flowers. You can craft these supports from various materials, including wood, metal, or creatively repurposed items. The charm of vertical climbing plants is not just in their growth habit but also in their ability to pair with ground-level companions. Picture cucumbers gracefully climbing a trellis, providing a canopy of shade to lettuce planted below, which thrives in cooler conditions.

Wall and Fence Planters: Walls and fences present an untapped potential for gardening. By attaching planters to these vertical surfaces, you can transform them into vibrant growing spaces. This technique is particularly suitable for herbs, small vegetables, and flowers, creating a living tapestry of greenery. The concept of a living wall takes this idea further, where modular planters are arranged artistically to grow plants that enjoy similar light and water conditions, resulting in an eye-catching and functional display.

The Charm of Hanging Baskets: Hanging baskets are a delightful way to add both decorative and functional elements to your garden. They are ideal for growing flowers, strawberries, and trailing herbs like thyme and rosemary, adding beauty and fragrance while conserving precious ground space. In hanging baskets, you can experiment with companion planting by combining plants with similar needs but different appearances, creating a varied and attractive display.

Innovative Use of Vertical Pallet Gardens: Pallets, often seen as mundane objects, can be upcycled into charming vertical gardens. They are great for growing lettuce, herbs, and small flowers. To ensure they are suitable for gardening, check that they haven't been chemically treated. You can paint or stain the pallets to complement your garden's aesthetic and fill the slats with soil and plants for a rustic yet organized vertical garden.

Maximizing Space with Tiered Planters and Shelves: Tiered planters and shelves are an excellent way to create layers of planting space, particularly effective for herb gardens or small vegetable patches. This approach allows you to strategically arrange plants based on their sunlight needs, with sun-loving plants at the top and those preferring shade at the bottom.

Utilizing Gutter Systems for Compact Gardening: Repurposed gutters attached to walls or beneath windows can be used for growing shallow-rooted plants like salad greens and strawberries. This setup can create a cascading effect of greenery, especially when each gutter section is used for different companion plants.

Considerations for Maintenance and Care: While vertical gardens offer many benefits, they also require thoughtful consideration in terms of maintenance and care. Accessibility is key — ensure that your vertical garden is easy to reach for tasks like watering, pruning, and harvesting. This not only makes garden care more convenient but also helps in closely monitoring the health of your plants.

Watering is a Special Focus in Vertical Gardening: Due to their exposure and the nature of their containers, vertical gardens may dry out faster than traditional ground-level beds. This necessitates more frequent watering to ensure plants stay hydrated. Implementing a drip irrigation system or a self-watering mechanism can be an efficient way to maintain consistent moisture levels, especially in taller installations.

The Aesthetic and Environmental Benefits: Vertical gardens don't just maximize space; they also bring a unique aesthetic value to your environment. They can turn bland walls into lush green spaces and add an element of beauty and tranquility to urban settings. Additionally, vertical gardens contribute positively to the environment by improving air quality and promoting biodiversity in urban areas.

Vertical gardening is more than just a space-saving technique; it's a creative and effective way to enhance the productivity and beauty of your gardening space. By incorporating vertical elements, you can transform even the smallest spaces into abundant and attractive green areas. It's a journey of exploring and utilizing vertical space, bringing a new dimension and perspective to the art of gardening. Whether you're an urban dweller with just a balcony or someone with a bit more space to experiment, vertical gardening offers a world of possibilities, making the sky quite literally the limit for your gardening aspirations.

Mutually Beneficial Plant Pairings

In companion gardening, the concept of mutually beneficial plant pairings forms the cornerstone of a thriving garden. This chapter, "Mutually Beneficial Plant Pairings," delves into the heart of companion planting, revealing the synergistic relationships between different plants and how they can enhance each other's growth, health, and yield.

The magic of companion planting lies in the understanding that some plants, when grown together, can offer remarkable benefits to each other. These benefits range from pest control and improved pollination to better nutrient uptake and enhanced growth rates. By pairing the right plants, gardeners can create a harmonious and productive ecosystem that is more resilient to environmental stresses.

In this chapter, we will explore:

- **Easy-to-Reference Charts and Lists:** Providing you with a handy guide to plant pairings, simplifying the process of planning your companion garden.

- **Maximizing Growth and Yield:** Understanding how certain plant combinations can result in a more bountiful harvest, offering practical examples and real-life success stories.

- **Natural Pest and Disease Control:** Exploring how some plants can protect their neighbors from pests and diseases, reducing the need for chemical interventions.

As we uncover these pairings, you'll gain insights into the subtle yet powerful interactions that occur in your garden. This knowledge is not only fascinating but also immensely practical, helping you create a garden that is both beautiful and abundant.

Whether you are a seasoned gardener or just starting, this chapter will equip you with the knowledge to make informed decisions about which plants to grow together for mutual benefit. Prepare to transform your garden into a space where plants not only coexist but thrive together in harmony and abundance.

Easy-to-Reference Charts and Lists

For gardeners, having an easy-to-reference guide to companion planting can be a game-changer. This subchapter provides you with concise charts and lists that serve as a quick reference for planning your garden. These resources simplify the process of determining which plants to grow together for mutual benefit.

Vegetable Companion Planting Chart

Vegetable	Good Companions	Bad Companions
Tomatoes	Basil, Marigold, Carrots	Cabbage, Fennel
Beans	Corn, Squash, Marigolds	Onions, Garlic
Peppers	Basil, Onions, Spinach	Beans, Kohlrabi
	Tomatoes,	Onions,
Carrots	Rosemary	Dill
Lettuce	Radishes, Strawberries	Broccoli, Cabbage
Cucumbers	Beans, Peas, Radishes	Aromatic herbs, Potatoes
Squash	Corn, Beans, Nasturtiums	Potatoes
	Carrots, Cucumbers,	
Peas	Radishes	Onions, Garlic, Leek
Broccoli	Dill, Chamomile, Rosemary	Strawberries, Tomatoes
Spinach	Strawberries, Fava beans	Potatoes

COMPANION PLANTING FOR BEGINNERS

Herb Companion Planting Chart

Herb	Good Companions	Bad Companions
Basil	Tomatoes, Peppers, Asparagus	Rue
Cilantro	Tomatoes, Peppers	Fennel
Dill	Cabbage, Onions, Lettuce	Carrots, Tomatoes
Rosemary	Beans, Cabbage, Carrots	Potatoes
Mint	Cabbage, Tomatoes	Parsley
Chives	Carrots, Tomatoes	Beans
Parsley	Tomatoes, Asparagus	Mint

Flower Companion Planting Chart

Flower	Good Companions	Bad Companions
Marigolds	Tomatoes, Peppers, Eggplants	-
Nasturtiums	Squash, Cucumbers, Radishes	-
Sunflowers	Corn, Cucumbers, Beans	Potatoes
Calendula	Tomatoes, Peppers, Asparagus	-
Lavender	Most vegetables and herbs	-

Key Tips for Using These Charts:

Using companion planting charts as a guide can significantly enhance the planning and success of your garden. These charts offer valuable insights into which plants thrive together and which might inhibit each other's growth. However, it's important to use these charts as a starting point and adapt their recommendations to your specific garden conditions. Let's delve deeper into key tips for effectively utilizing these charts in your companion gardening strategy.

Understanding Complementarity in Plant Needs:

Each plant has its unique requirements for water, sunlight, and soil type. Companion planting charts help identify pairs or groups of plants that have similar or complementary needs. For example, pairing plants that all prefer full sun and moderate watering can create a harmonious garden spot.

Some plants can positively influence the soil conditions for their neighbors. For instance, legumes fix nitrogen in the soil, benefiting nearby nitrogen-loving plants.

Spacing for Healthy Growth:

Proper spacing is crucial in companion planting. Plants need enough room to grow without competing for resources. Overcrowded plants can become stressed, making them more susceptible to pests and diseases.

Adequate space allows each plant to receive the sunlight, air circulation, and nutrients it needs. This not only improves plant health but can also lead to a more productive garden.

The Importance of Crop Rotation:

Repeatedly growing the same type of plant in the same spot can deplete the soil of specific nutrients. Rotating companion plantings helps maintain soil fertility and balance.

Many pests and diseases are plant-specific. By rotating plants, you disrupt the life cycle of these pests and reduce the likelihood of recurring disease issues.

Using Companion Planting Charts as a Guide:

While these charts provide general guidelines, it's important to observe and adapt to how different pairings perform in your specific garden environment. Factors like local climate, soil conditions, and individual plant varieties can influence the success of companion planting.

Feel free to experiment with different combinations and observe the results. Gardening is a learning process, and sometimes the most successful pairings are discovered through trial and error.

Additional Considerations:

Consider how the changing seasons affect the plants in your garden. Some plants may be more compatible at different times of the year.

Use companion planting to naturally repel pests or attract beneficial insects, but also be vigilant about monitoring for any issues that arise.

Companion planting charts are a valuable tool in creating a harmonious and productive garden. By understanding and applying the principles of complementarity, spacing, and rotation, and by adapting these guidelines to your specific garden conditions, you can enhance the health and yield of your plants. Remember, gardening is as much an art as it is a science. Using these charts as a foundational guide while being open to experimentation and observation can lead to a more vibrant, resilient, and bountiful garden. The goal is to create a dynamic ecosystem where plants support and benefit each other, contributing to a sustainable and enjoyable gardening experience.

Maximizing Growth and Yield

Achieving a bountiful harvest is a primary goal for many gardeners, and companion planting can play a significant role in maximizing both growth and yield. Now we focuses on how to strategically pair plants to enhance their productivity, drawing upon the principles of companion planting to create a flourishing garden.

Understanding Synergistic Relationships:

Understanding synergistic relationships in companion gardening is about recognizing and utilizing the natural interactions between different plants to create a more productive and healthy garden. These relationships go beyond mere coexistence; they involve a mutualistic interaction where plants significantly benefit each other. Let's explore this concept more deeply, using the classic example of corn and beans, and how understanding these relationships can inform your garden planning.

Corn and Beans: A Classic Example of Plant Synergy

Beans, being legumes, have a unique ability to fix atmospheric nitrogen into the soil through a symbiotic relationship with nitrogen-fixing bacteria in their root nodules. This process enriches the soil with nitrogen, a vital nutrient for plant growth.

In return, the tall and sturdy stalks of corn provide a natural trellis for climbing bean plants. This support is crucial for the growth habit of many bean varieties, allowing them to receive more sunlight and air circulation, which can lead to a healthier plant and better yields.

This relationship is mutually beneficial. Beans improve soil fertility, which is advantageous for the corn, while corn provides the necessary support for beans to thrive. This symbiotic relationship reduces the need for artificial fertilizers and trellising materials.

Planning a Garden Based on Synergistic Relationships

When planning your garden, consider what each plant needs and what it can offer to its companions. For example, some plants may repel pests that commonly affect another plant, or some may attract beneficial insects that help pollinate another crop.

Look for combinations where the growth habit or needs of one plant complement the other. Besides the corn and beans example, consider pairings like tomatoes and basil, where basil's strong scent repels pests that commonly affect tomatoes.

Synergistic relationships can also help in optimizing space. Vertical climbers can be paired with low-growing, ground-cover plants. This not only maximizes the use of space but can also create a microclimate that benefits both plants.

Building a Garden Ecosystem

By understanding and implementing synergistic relationships, you're not just growing plants side by side; you're building an ecosystem where each plant contributes to the health and productivity of others.

These relationships can reduce the need for chemical inputs, as natural plant interactions take over the roles of pest control and fertilization. This approach leads to a more sustainable and environmentally friendly garden.

While there are well-known synergistic pairings, there's also room for experimentation. Observe how different plants interact in your garden and be open to trying new combinations. What works in one climate or soil type may not work in another, so adaptability is key.

Holistic Approach to Garden Planning:

When planning your garden layout, think of it as a holistic system where each plant plays a role. This approach can lead to a garden that is not only productive but also more resilient to pests and diseases.

Incorporate the concept of successional planting to maintain synergy throughout the growing season. As one crop finishes, another can take its place, continuing the beneficial relationships.

While diversity is beneficial, it's also important to ensure that the plants you choose to grow together are compatible. For example, plants that require similar soil pH or moisture levels can be good companions.

Understanding and utilizing synergistic relationships in companion gardening is a powerful way to enhance the overall health, productivity, and sustainability of your garden. By carefully selecting and positioning plants that benefit each other, you can create a thriving garden ecosystem that is greater than the sum of its parts. This approach not only yields a bountiful harvest but also contributes to a more balanced and natural gardening experience.

Enhancing Soil Health and Nutrient Availability:

Enhancing soil health and nutrient availability is a cornerstone of successful gardening, particularly in companion planting where the interaction between different plants can significantly impact the soil's quality. One of the key elements of this interaction is the role of nitrogen-fixing plants in enriching the soil, thereby benefiting their neighboring plants. Let's explore this concept in greater detail.

Nitrogen-Fixing Plants: Nature's Fertilizers

Legumes, such as peas and beans, play a special role in soil enhancement. They have a symbiotic relationship with nitrogen-fixing bacteria (Rhizobia) in their root nodules. These bacteria have the unique ability to convert atmospheric nitrogen into a form that is usable by plants – a process known as nitrogen fixation.

As legumes grow, they increase the nitrogen content in the soil. This is especially beneficial in soils that are depleted of nutrients. When legumes are harvested or die, the nitrogen stored in their roots and plant tissue becomes available to subsequent plants, enriching the soil.

Pairing Nitrogen-Fixers with Nitrogen-Loving Plants

Pairing nitrogen-fixing plants with those that thrive on nitrogen, such as leafy greens (e.g., lettuce, spinach, and kale), can lead to more vigorous growth and higher yields. The nitrogen released by legumes is readily available for these companion plants, providing them with a critical nutrient for their growth.

This pairing not only benefits the current plants but also contributes to the long-term health of the soil. With each growing season, nitrogen-fixing plants can help replenish and maintain the soil's fertility, reducing the need for synthetic fertilizers.

Strategies for Maximizing Benefits

Implementing crop rotation with legumes can enhance soil health over larger garden areas. For example, rotating a legume crop with a leafy green crop can help ensure that different parts of the garden benefit from the nitrogen-fixing abilities of legumes.

Interplanting legumes with nitrogen-loving plants is an effective way to maximize space and soil benefits. Additionally, using legumes as cover crops during the off-season can protect and enrich the soil.

Observation and Adaptation

The effectiveness of nitrogen-fixing plants can vary depending on local soil conditions. Regular soil testing can provide insights into nutrient levels and help tailor your companion planting strategy.

COMPANION PLANTING FOR BEGINNERS

Different plants have varying nitrogen requirements. Understanding these needs can help you make informed decisions about pairing plants for optimal growth.

Enhancing soil health and nutrient availability through the strategic use of nitrogen-fixing plants like legumes is a sustainable and efficient way to enrich your garden soil. This practice not only leads to healthier, more productive plants but also contributes to the overall ecological balance of your garden, promoting a cycle of growth and renewal that benefits all plants within the ecosystem.

Natural Pest Management:

Natural pest management is an integral component of sustainable gardening practices, particularly in companion planting, where the strategic placement of certain plants can significantly diminish pest problems. This approach harnesses the natural properties of plants to deter pests, thereby reducing the reliance on chemical pesticides and promoting a healthier, more balanced garden ecosystem. Let's delve deeper into how companion plants contribute to natural pest control and the broader benefits of this approach.

Utilizing Companion Plants for Pest Control:

Marigolds are a prime example of natural pest deterrents. They release a substance from their roots that is toxic to nematodes – microscopic worms that can damage the roots of vegetable plants like tomatoes, causing stunted growth and reduced yields. Planting marigolds around or in rotation with susceptible vegetables can significantly reduce nematode populations in the soil.

Different companion plants can deter various pests. For instance, basil emits a strong scent that repels thrips, flies, and mosquitoes, making it a great companion for plants that are susceptible to these pests. Similarly, plants like lavender and chives can repel aphids and Japanese beetles.

Enhanced Plant Growth and Fruit Production:

When plants are not under constant stress from pest attacks, they can allocate more energy towards growth and fruit production. This leads to healthier plants with potentially higher yields.

Natural pest control contributes to the overall health of plants. Healthy plants are more resistant to diseases and can better withstand occasional pest pressures.

Creating a Balanced Ecosystem:

Some companion plants can attract beneficial insects, such as ladybugs, lacewings, and bees, which play a crucial role in controlling pest populations and pollinating plants. For example, flowering plants like dill and fennel attract ladybugs that feed on aphids.

A diverse garden with a variety of plants can create a more balanced ecosystem, making it less susceptible to large-scale pest infestations. Diversity can disrupt the habitat preferences of certain pests, reducing their likelihood of establishing a significant presence.

Integrating Companion Planting into Garden Design:

Consider the placement of pest-repellent plants in proximity to susceptible crops. For example, planting garlic near roses can help deter aphids from the roses, while nasturtiums planted around squash can repel squash bugs.

Interplanting pest-repellent plants among your crops can provide widespread protection. This method ensures that the beneficial properties of these plants are spread throughout the garden, offering a more comprehensive defense against pests.

Eco-Friendly and Sustainable Approach:

By relying on the natural pest-repellent properties of plants, gardeners can minimize or even eliminate the need for chemical pesticides. This approach not only protects the environment but also ensures that the produce from the garden is free from chemical residues.

COMPANION PLANTING FOR BEGINNERS

Natural pest management practices contribute to the long-term health of the soil. Chemical pesticides can sometimes harm beneficial soil organisms and disrupt the soil's natural balance, but using companion plants maintains a healthy soil ecosystem.

Observation and Adaptation:

Regularly monitor the garden for pest activity and adjust your companion planting strategy as needed. The effectiveness of certain plant combinations can vary based on local conditions and pest populations.

Gardening is often about trial and error. Experiment with different companion plant combinations to see which works best for your specific garden conditions and pest challenges.

Natural pest management through companion planting is a holistic and effective approach to maintaining a healthy and productive garden. By understanding and utilizing the pest-repellent properties of certain plants, gardeners can create a more balanced and sustainable garden ecosystem. This method not only enhances plant growth and fruit production but also contributes to the overall health of the garden environment, promoting a natural cycle of growth and protection.

Improved Pollination:

Improved pollination is a vital aspect of a healthy and productive garden, particularly in the context of producing fruits and seeds. Pollinators play a crucial role in this process, and attracting a diverse array of these beneficial creatures can significantly boost your garden's productivity. In companion gardening, the strategic inclusion of flowering plants can create an environment that not only supports pollination but also enhances the overall health and aesthetic appeal of the garden. Let's explore this topic in more depth.

The Role of Pollinators in the Garden:

Pollinators like bees, butterflies, birds, and even some types of beetles and flies, are responsible for transferring pollen from one flower to another, facilitating the fertilization process. This process is crucial for the formation of fruits and seeds in many plants, particularly in fruit and vegetable gardening.

A diverse range of plants in the garden attracts a wider variety of pollinators. Different pollinators are attracted to different types of flowers, so having a variety of flowering plants can ensure more comprehensive pollination coverage for your garden.

Incorporating Flowering Plants for Attracting Pollinators:

Choose a variety of flowering plants that bloom at different times throughout the growing season. This ensures a continuous supply of flowers, providing nectar and pollen for pollinators from early spring to late fall.

Integrate flowering plants into your vegetable garden as companions. For example, planting marigolds or nasturtiums among vegetables not only adds color and beauty to your garden but also attracts pollinators and can even deter certain pests.

Beyond just planting flowers, consider creating habitats that are conducive to pollinators. This includes providing sources of water, shelter, and nesting sites. For example, leaving a part of your garden a little wild can create a habitat for native bees.

Benefits of Improved Pollination:

Enhanced pollination leads to more effective fertilization, resulting in a higher yield of fruits and seeds from your plants. Better pollination can also improve the size, uniformity, and even taste of the fruits and vegetables produced.

Attracting natural pollinators helps reduce the need for manual pollination or reliance on declining wild pollinator populations. It supports biodiversity and contributes to the ecological balance in and around your garden.

Tips for Maximizing Pollination:

Grouping the same types of flowers together can make them more attractive and visible to pollinators. If possible, avoid or minimize the use of pesticides, especially during flowering, as they can harm pollinators. Opt for natural or organic pest control methods.Native plants are often well-suited to local pollinators and can be more resilient to local pests and diseases.

In conclusion, improved pollination through diverse plantings and the incorporation of flowering plants is not only beneficial for fruit and seed production but also for the overall health and ecological balance of your garden. By creating a pollinator-friendly environment, you not only enhance the productivity and beauty of your garden but also contribute to the preservation and support of vital pollinator populations.

Optimizing Space and Resources:

Optimizing space and resources is a fundamental principle of effective gardening, particularly important in companion planting. This approach allows gardeners to maximize the utility of their available garden space, leading to increased productivity and efficiency. By understanding and leveraging the different growth habits and needs of various plants, gardeners can create a harmonious and densely planted garden that yields more than the sum of its parts. Let's explore this concept in more depth.

Efficient Use of Space Through Companion Planting:

One of the key strategies in companion planting for space optimization involves pairing plants with different root depths. For example, shallow-rooted herbs can be planted next to deeper-rooted vegetables. This means that plants are not competing for the same nutrients and water levels, allowing for more efficient use of the soil. Herbs like basil or parsley can be planted alongside tomatoes or carrots, making full use of both the upper and lower soil layers.

Utilizing plants with different growth habits – such as vertical climbers alongside low-growing crops – maximizes the use of both vertical and horizontal space. For instance, planting beans, which climb upwards, next to sprawling plants like squash, ensures that both types of plants have the space they need to thrive without competing with each other.

COMPANION PLANTING FOR BEGINNERS

Higher Overall Yield from Efficient Planting:

By arranging plants strategically based on their size, growth pattern, and root structure, you can fit a greater variety of plants into a given area. This not only maximizes the productivity of your garden space but also can lead to a more continuous and varied harvest throughout the growing season.

When plants are chosen and positioned to complement each other, there is less competition for essential resources like sunlight, water, and soil nutrients. This symbiotic relationship often results in healthier plants and, consequently, a higher overall yield.

Other Benefits of Space and Resource Optimization:

Close planting of companion species can create beneficial microclimates. For example, taller plants can provide necessary shade to more heat-sensitive understory plants, reducing water evaporation and protecting them from intense sun.

Companion planting can also lead to improved soil conditions. As different plants have varying nutrient requirements and contributions, they can help maintain a balanced soil ecology, reducing the need for artificial fertilizers.

Efficient use of space can also aid in pest and disease control. For instance, planting garlic or onions around susceptible plants can help deter certain pests, reducing the need for chemical controls and leading to a more natural garden ecosystem.

Considerations for Optimizing Space:

Thoughtful planning is key. Consider the mature size of plants, their sunlight and water requirements, and their compatibility with neighboring plants.

This involves planting a new crop immediately after one has been harvested. It's an effective way to keep the garden productive throughout the growing season. For example, once spring peas are harvested, the same space can be used for a summer crop like beans.

COMPANION PLANTING FOR BEGINNERS

Planting different crops in close proximity can be highly beneficial. For instance, fast-growing, short-lived plants like lettuce can be planted between slower-growing, long-term crops like broccoli. The lettuce will be harvested before the broccoli needs the extra space.

The strategic use of companion planting to optimize space and resources is a key element in creating a productive and sustainable garden. By carefully considering plant characteristics and their interactions, gardeners can maximize the output and health of their garden, even within limited spaces. This approach not only enhances yield but also contributes to a diverse and ecologically balanced garden environment.

Microclimate Management:

Microclimate management through companion planting is a sophisticated gardening strategy that involves manipulating the local growing environment to benefit the plants. By thoughtfully positioning certain plants together, gardeners can create microclimates within their gardens, which can protect more vulnerable plants from harsh conditions and improve overall plant health and productivity. Let's delve deeper into how tall plants and ground cover crops can be used to manage microclimates effectively.

Creating Shade and Protecting Sun-Sensitive Plants:

Tall plants like sunflowers or corn naturally cast shade with their broad leaves and tall stalks. When strategically placed, they can shield lower-growing, sun-sensitive plants from the intense midday sun. This is particularly beneficial in hot climates or during the peak of summer when the sun can stress plants and evaporate soil moisture quickly.

Plants that thrive in partial shade or that are prone to wilting under strong sunlight, such as lettuce or spinach, can greatly benefit from the shade provided by taller plants. This arrangement can lead to more robust growth and can extend the harvesting period of cool-weather crops that might otherwise bolt or wither in too much heat.

Ground Cover Crops for Soil Temperature and Moisture Regulation:

Low-growing ground cover crops, such as clover or creeping thyme, can play a critical role in regulating soil temperature and moisture. By covering the soil, they help retain moisture and keep the soil cooler, which is beneficial for most plants during hot weather.

In addition to moderating soil temperature and moisture, ground cover crops can also help prevent soil erosion, particularly in areas prone to heavy rains or winds. Their dense growth habit can suppress weeds, reducing competition for nutrients and water.

Other Considerations in Microclimate Management:

Tall plants or densely planted hedges can act as windbreaks, protecting the rest of the garden from strong winds that can dry out soil and damage delicate plants.

Plants with large leaves, such as squash or zucchini, can help maintain higher humidity levels around them, which can be beneficial for plants that thrive in more humid conditions.

Adapting to Your Garden's Needs:

Each garden is unique, and microclimate management should be adapted to its specific conditions. Regular observation of how different plants react to their placement can provide insights into how best to use tall plants and ground covers for microclimate management.

The needs of your garden may change from year to year or even within a single growing season. Being flexible and willing to rearrange plants or try different combinations is key to effectively managing microclimates.

Microclimate management through the strategic use of companion planting is a powerful tool in the gardener's toolkit. By understanding and utilizing the natural properties of tall plants for shading and ground covers for soil temperature and moisture regulation, gardeners can create more favorable growing conditions within their gardens. This approach not only enhances plant growth and yield but also contributes to a more resilient and sustainable garden ecosystem.

Crop Rotation and Companion Planting:

Crop rotation in conjunction with companion planting is an advanced gardening technique that enhances soil health, mitigates pest and disease problems, and optimizes nutrient availability. This practice involves changing the position of crops and their companions in the garden each year. Let's delve deeper into how this strategy works and the benefits it offers.

Breaking Pest and Disease Cycles:

Many pests and diseases are specific to certain types of plants. By rotating crops, you disrupt the habitat that these pests and diseases have come to rely on. For example, if a particular soil-borne disease affected tomatoes one year, planting tomatoes in a different location the next year can help avoid a repeat infestation.

Crop rotation also limits the spread of diseases. Soil-borne pathogens tend to accumulate in soil where the same crop is planted year after year. Rotating crops helps to reduce the concentration of these pathogens.

Maintaining Soil Fertility:

Different plants have varying nutrient requirements and uptake patterns. By rotating crops, you can prevent specific nutrients from being continuously depleted in the same area of soil. For instance, heavy feeders like tomatoes can be followed by nitrogen-fixing legumes, which help replenish nitrogen levels in the soil.

Different crops also contribute to soil structure in various ways. Deep-rooted plants can help break up compact soil and improve aeration, while others might contribute organic matter to the soil.

Integrating Companion Planting with Crop Rotation:

Rotating companion plantings further enhances soil health. Companion plants often bring additional benefits such as pest deterrence or soil enrichment, and rotating these pairings can provide these benefits to different areas of the garden over time.

This practice contributes to a more diverse and balanced garden ecosystem. Diversity in planting discourages monoculture-related problems and encourages a more resilient garden environment.

Practical Considerations in Crop Rotation:

Effective crop rotation requires planning and keeping track of what was planted where in previous years. This information is crucial for deciding the rotation plan for the upcoming season.

It's important to rotate crops by plant family, not just individual species. For example, avoid planting crops from the Solanaceae family (tomatoes, peppers, eggplants) in the same bed year after year.

Be adaptable with your rotation plan. Sometimes, unexpected factors like weather conditions or pest outbreaks may require a change in your planned rotations.

Integrating crop rotation with companion planting is a dynamic and effective approach to garden management. It not only helps in controlling pests and diseases and maintaining soil health but also contributes to a more sustainable and productive garden. By thoughtfully planning your garden layout and being attentive to the history of your plantings, you can maximize the benefits of this time-tested agricultural practice.

Observing and Adapting:

Observation and adaptation are fundamental practices in the art and science of gardening, especially in the context of companion planting. They involve closely monitoring the growth, health, and interactions of your plants, and then using this information to inform and refine your gardening strategies. Let's delve deeper into these crucial components of successful gardening.

COMPANION PLANTING FOR BEGINNERS

The Importance of Observing Your Garden:

Regularly observing your plants can reveal a lot about their health and the overall balance of your garden. Pay attention to changes in leaf color, growth patterns, and signs of stress or disease. For example, if certain plants consistently underperform or seem prone to disease, it may indicate a problem with the soil, water, light, or their companion plants.

Companion planting is based on the principle that certain plants can benefit each other when grown together. By observing how plants interact in your garden, you can learn which combinations are most effective. Do they seem to grow better or worse when planted near each other? Are there signs of competition or mutual support?

Recording Observations:

Maintain a record of what you plant and where, along with notes on their progress, weather conditions, and any issues that arise. This record-keeping can be invaluable for planning future gardens and understanding long-term trends in your garden.

Taking regular photos of your garden can provide a visual record of changes over time and can help you spot issues you might otherwise miss.

Adapting Based on Observations:

Use the insights gained from your observations to make changes in your garden. This might involve altering the placement of plants, changing watering or feeding practices, or trying different plant combinations.

Gardening often involves trial and error. Don't be afraid to experiment with new techniques or plant pairings based on your observations. What works in one garden or for one gardener may not work in another, so personal experimentation is key.

Learning from Experiences:

At the end of each growing season, review your notes and consider what worked well and what didn't. This reflection can guide your planning for the next season.

Gardens are dynamic systems influenced by many variables, including weather patterns, soil conditions, and pest populations. Be prepared to adapt your gardening practices as these conditions change.

Observing and adapting are ongoing processes that are essential to developing a thriving garden. They require patience, attention to detail, and a willingness to learn and change. By becoming attuned to the needs and behaviors of your plants and being flexible in your approach, you can create a garden that is not only productive but also a source of continuous learning and enjoyment.

By applying these principles, you can significantly enhance the growth and yield of your garden. Companion planting is about creating a balanced ecosystem where plants support each other, leading to a more productive and sustainable garden.

Preventing Pests and Diseases Naturally

A key benefit of companion planting is its ability to help manage pests and diseases in a natural and sustainable way. This subchapter delves into how strategic plant pairings and garden practices can significantly reduce the incidence of pests and diseases, eliminating the need for harsh chemical treatments and fostering a healthier, more balanced garden ecosystem.

Natural Pest Repellents:

- Many plants have natural pest-repelling properties. For example, marigolds release a substance that deters nematodes, while the strong scents of herbs like lavender, rosemary, and basil can repel a variety of insects.

- Planting these natural repellents near susceptible crops can protect them from pest infestations.

Attracting Beneficial Insects:

- Certain plants attract beneficial insects, which are natural predators to common garden pests. For instance, flowering plants like dill and fennel attract ladybugs that feed on aphids.

- Integrating these plants into your garden helps maintain a natural balance and reduces the need for insecticides.

Physical Barriers:

- Use physical barriers such as row covers to protect plants from pests. This can be particularly effective for young plants that are more vulnerable to insect damage.

- Ensure proper ventilation under covers to prevent overheating and humidity buildup, which can lead to disease.

Healthy Soil for Disease Prevention:

- Healthy soil is the foundation of a healthy garden. Incorporate organic matter and practice crop rotation to maintain soil health and prevent disease.

- Companion planting can also improve soil structure and nutrient availability, further supporting plant health.

Diversity to Outsmart Pests:

- A diverse garden is less appealing to pests and more resilient to disease. Plant a mix of vegetables, herbs, and flowers to create a less targeted environment for pests.

- Diversity also ensures that if one plant type is affected by a pest or disease, it doesn't spread easily to others.

Trap Cropping:

- Plant trap crops that are more attractive to pests than your main crops. For example, planting nasturtiums to attract aphids away from vegetables.

- Once the trap crop is infested, it can be removed and disposed of, keeping pests away from your main crops.

Regular Monitoring and Maintenance:

- Regularly inspect your plants for signs of pests and diseases. Early detection is key to managing problems before they become severe.

- Remove any diseased or infested plant material promptly to prevent the spread.

Promoting Air Circulation:

- Arrange plants to ensure good air circulation. This helps reduce fungal diseases, as many thrive in stagnant, humid conditions.

- Prune plants as needed to improve airflow.

Through these natural methods, you can effectively manage pests and diseases in your companion garden, fostering a more sustainable and ecologically balanced environment. This approach not only benefits your plants but also contributes to the overall health of your local ecosystem.

Top Five Companion Plants

This subchapter delves into the top five companion plants, offering insights and practical recommendations to enhance your companion gardening experience. These plant pairings are not only beneficial for increasing yield and deterring pests but also contribute to the overall health and balance of your garden. Let's explore each of these top companions and understand why they are so effective.

COMPANION PLANTING FOR BEGINNERS

1. Beans and Peas: The Nitrogen Fixers

Beans and peas are invaluable in a companion garden, especially when planted near nitrogen-loving plants. These legumes have a unique ability to fix atmospheric nitrogen into the soil, making it available for nearby plants. This feature is particularly beneficial for green leafy vegetables like Swiss chard, kale, lettuce, and spinach, which thrive on nitrogen to develop their lush green foliage.

Once beans and peas complete their life cycle, their remains, including roots and leaves, can be worked back into the soil. This practice enriches the soil with a natural, potent source of nitrogen, reducing the need for artificial fertilizers.

2. Alliums: The Pest Deterrents

The Allium family, which includes onions, garlic, leeks, shallots, and chives, plays a dual role in the garden. Not only do these plants take up minimal space, allowing for efficient use of garden areas, but they also act as powerful pest deterrents. Their strong scent and taste repel a range of pests such as rabbits, cabbage worms, and Japanese beetles, making them ideal companions for brassicas (kale, broccoli, cauliflower, bok choy, cabbage) and other vegetables like tomatoes, carrots, and celery.

3. Marigolds: The Natural Pesticide

Marigolds, particularly the French variety, are often referred to as the 'wonder drug' of the companion planting world. These vibrant flowers release a pesticide chemical from their roots that remains active even years after the plant is gone. Effective against a host of garden pests like nematodes, beetles, and squash bugs, marigolds are excellent companions for brassicas and cucurbits (cucumbers, squash, melons). They are easy to start in small spaces and can be moved around the garden in simple containers to maximize their pest-repelling effect.

4. Herbs: Flavor Enhancers and Pest Repellers

Herbs such as basil, rosemary, thyme, and sage are not just culinary delights but also valuable companions for tomato plants. Known to enhance the flavor of tomatoes, these herbs also repel hornworms, mosquitoes, and flies. Planting them at the base of tomato plants maximizes garden space and provides a dual benefit of flavorful herbs and healthier tomato plants.

5. Radishes: The Quick Harvest

Radishes are the garden's time managers. They are perfect for planting alongside slow-growing plants like eggplants and peppers. Radishes grow quickly, allowing you to harvest them before their companions take up more space. This efficient use of time and space makes radishes an ideal choice for maximizing garden yields. Additionally, radishes are known to deter squash borers, offering protection to vulnerable squash plants.

Companion planting is a dynamic and rewarding approach to gardening. By understanding the unique benefits each plant brings to the table, gardeners can create a harmonious and productive garden. Remember, a successful garden is not just about what you plant, but also about how you plant them together. So, embrace these companion planting tips and watch as your garden flourishes with health, abundance, and diversity.

DOWNLOAD YOUR EXCLUSIVE BONUSES

Advanced Companion Gardening Strategies

After mastering the basics of companion gardening, it's time to elevate your skills with advanced strategies. This chapter is designed for those who are ready to deepen their understanding and take their gardens to the next level. Here, we explore sophisticated techniques that can further enhance the efficiency, productivity, and sustainability of your companion garden.

Advanced companion gardening goes beyond just knowing which plants grow well together. It involves a deeper understanding of ecological relationships, soil health, microclimates, and long-term garden planning. This chapter will introduce you to concepts and practices that are less commonly known but incredibly effective in maximizing the potential of your garden space.

In this chapter, we will cover:

- **Beyond the Basics: Intermediate Tips and Tricks:** Refine your gardening techniques with nuanced tips that can make a significant difference in plant health and yield.

- **Incorporating Cover Crops in Home Gardens:** Learn how cover crops can improve soil fertility, control pests, and enhance overall garden health.

•**Organic and Sustainable Practices:** Delve deeper into sustainable practices that not only benefit your garden but also contribute to environmental conservation.

This journey into advanced companion gardening will require patience, observation, and a willingness to experiment. But the rewards are plentiful - a garden that is a true testament to the principles of ecology and sustainability, one that thrives in harmony with nature.

Whether you're looking to increase your harvest, create a more resilient garden ecosystem, or simply enjoy the deeper nuances of gardening, this chapter will provide you with the knowledge and tools to achieve your goals.

Beyond the Basics: Intermediate Tips and Tricks

Now that you're comfortable with the fundamentals of companion gardening, it's time to explore some intermediate tips and tricks that can further enhance your garden's productivity and sustainability. This subchapter presents a collection of nuanced strategies for those looking to refine their companion gardening skills.

1. Succession Planting:

Stagger Plantings: Staggered planting, also known as succession planting, is a highly effective gardening technique that maximizes the productivity and extends the harvest period of your garden. Instead of planting all your crops at once, staggered planting involves sowing seeds or planting seedlings at regular intervals. This approach ensures a continuous supply of produce throughout the growing season, providing fresh vegetables and herbs for your table over an extended period, rather than all at once.

In a traditional garden setup, planting all crops simultaneously can lead to a situation where everything matures at the same time. This often results in a surplus or glut, where you have more produce than you can use, preserve, or give away. Staggered planting helps avoid this by spreading out the harvest over several weeks or months. For example, if you plant a row of lettuce every two weeks instead of all at once, you will have a fresh supply of lettuce throughout the season instead of a single large harvest.

Careful planning is key to successful staggered planting. Consider the growth rate and maturity time of each crop. Fast-growing vegetables like radishes or lettuce are ideal for staggered planting as they mature quickly. You can also plan for a continuous harvest by planting varieties with different maturity dates. For instance, planting early, mid-season, and late varieties of tomatoes can provide you with a steady supply of tomatoes rather than a single large harvest.

Staggered planting can also contribute to better pest and disease management. By avoiding a large, dense crop of the same plant, you reduce the risk of diseases or pests wiping out your entire harvest. This method can also lead to more efficient use of space in the garden. As early crops are harvested, space is freed up for planting later-season crops, allowing for a fuller utilization of the garden area throughout the growing season.

Staggered planting can be adjusted based on weather conditions and climate. In areas with a short growing season, starting some crops indoors can extend the growing period. In contrast, in warmer climates with a longer growing season, you have more flexibility with timing.

Rotating the types of crops planted in succession can help maintain soil health. Different plants have varying nutrient needs and contributions, and rotating them can prevent nutrient depletion in the soil.

In conclusion, staggered planting is an efficient way to manage your garden's productivity, ensuring that you can enjoy fresh produce throughout the growing season. This method requires thoughtful planning and monitoring but pays off in the form of a prolonged and more manageable harvest, better pest and disease control, and optimal use of garden space.

Companion Succession is an innovative approach in gardening that combines the principles of succession planting and companion planting. This method involves planning your planting schedule so that as one crop finishes its growing cycle, it is followed by another that not only thrives in the subsequent conditions but also maintains or enhances the companionship benefits. An example of this would be following early spring greens with heat-loving tomatoes. Let's delve into how this method works and its benefits.

Spring greens, such as lettuce, spinach, and kale, are cool-weather crops that grow well in the mild temperatures of early spring. They have relatively short growing cycles and are typically ready for harvest before the heat of summer sets in. Once these greens are harvested, the space can be used for planting summer crops like tomatoes. This transition takes advantage of the changing seasonal conditions – from the cooler temperatures of spring to the warmer temperatures ideal for tomatoes.

This approach allows each plant to grow in its preferred environmental conditions, thereby maximizing yield and reducing the likelihood of plant stress and disease.

Different plants have varying effects on soil health. Leafy greens often have shallow roots and can help prepare the soil for deeper-rooted plants like tomatoes. Additionally, the leafy greens can help suppress weeds and keep the soil cool and moist, which can be beneficial for the tomato plants that follow.

Rotating different families of plants can help break cycles of pests and diseases. For instance, certain pests or diseases may target greens but not tomatoes, and vice versa. By rotating these crops, you can reduce the chances of reinfestation or disease carryover.

Effective companion succession requires careful planning, especially in terms of timing. You need to ensure that the transition between crops is seamless and that the second crop is planted at the right time for optimal growth.

After harvesting the spring greens, it might be beneficial to amend the soil before planting tomatoes. This replenishment can include adding compost or other organic matter to ensure that the tomatoes have the nutrients they need to thrive.

In summary, companion succession planting, such as transitioning from early spring greens to tomatoes, is a strategic way to maximize garden space and productivity. It takes into account the different needs and benefits of each plant, ensuring a healthy, bountiful garden throughout the growing season.

2. Interplanting and Intercropping:

Mixed Planting: a technique that involves growing quick-maturing crops alongside slower-growing ones, is an excellent strategy for maximizing space efficiency and maintaining healthy soil in your garden. This approach allows gardeners to make the most out of their available space by planting fast-growing vegetables, such as radishes or lettuce, in proximity to slower-maturing crops like broccoli.

The benefits of mixed planting are multifaceted.

By interplanting quick-growing crops between slower ones, you utilize the space that would otherwise remain unproductive for a significant period. For example, radishes can be harvested within a few weeks of planting, well before broccoli reaches maturity.

Keeping the soil covered with plants is beneficial for its health. The quick-growing plants protect the soil from erosion, maintain better moisture levels, and can even help suppress weeds that would otherwise compete with the slower-growing crops.

This planting method also provides a continuous harvest. As you pick the fast-maturing vegetables, the slower ones are still developing, ensuring a steady supply of produce from the same plot.

Mixed planting is an efficient and effective way to get the most out of your gardening space, promoting both productivity and soil health.

Strategic Intercropping is a smart gardening technique that involves planting different crops in close proximity for mutual benefit, particularly regarding pest management and soil health improvement. A classic example of this method is pairing nitrogen-fixing plants with heavy-feeding crops.

Nitrogen-fixing plants, such as beans and peas, have the ability to convert atmospheric nitrogen into a form that is usable by plants. This process enriches the soil with nitrogen, which is essential for the growth of heavy feeders like corn or tomatoes.

Intercropping can also help in reducing pest populations naturally. Certain plants can deter pests from their neighbors or attract beneficial insects that prey on common pests.

This technique allows for the efficient use of garden space. While the nitrogen-fixers are growing and enriching the soil, the heavy feeders are taking advantage of the increased nutrient availability.

The varied root systems of intercropped plants can enhance soil structure and aeration, promoting a healthier soil ecosystem.

Strategic intercropping is an effective way to enhance soil fertility and manage pests naturally. By understanding the complementary needs and benefits of different plants, gardeners can create a more productive and sustainable gardening environment.

3. Soil Health Monitoring:

Regular Soil Testing is a crucial practice for any gardener aiming to maintain optimal growing conditions in their garden. It involves periodically analyzing the soil to assess its nutrient content, pH level, and overall health. This practice enables gardeners to make informed decisions about planting and soil amendments, ensuring that the soil provides the ideal environment for plant growth.

Soil tests reveal essential information about nutrient levels, including deficiencies or excesses of key elements like nitrogen, phosphorus, and potassium. Based on these results, gardeners can tailor their fertilization strategies to meet the specific needs of their plants, avoiding under or over-fertilization.

COMPANION PLANTING FOR BEGINNERS

The pH level of the soil significantly affects plant growth. Soil testing helps in identifying the pH level and allows gardeners to adjust it through amendments like lime or sulfur to create the ideal conditions for their plants.

Understanding soil health enables gardeners to choose plants that are best suited to their garden's specific conditions or to adjust the soil to accommodate a wider variety of plants.

Regular testing allows gardeners to use fertilizers and amendments more efficiently, reducing waste and minimizing environmental impact.

Regular soil testing is a vital tool for maintaining a healthy and productive garden. It provides valuable insights into the soil's condition, guiding gardeners in making precise adjustments to their planting and soil management strategies, ultimately ensuring the long-term health and sustainability of their garden ecosystem.

Companion Plants for Soil Improvement: Incorporating companion plants like comfrey and borage into your garden can significantly improve soil health, thanks to their deep-root systems. These plants are not only beneficial in themselves but also play a crucial role in enhancing the growth and health of neighboring plants.

Comfrey and borage have deep root systems that reach into the subsoil layers, accessing nutrients that are beyond the reach of shallower-rooted plants. They bring these nutrients up to the surface layers of the soil, making them accessible to neighboring plants.

The deep roots of these plants help to break up compact soil, improving aeration and water penetration. This can be especially beneficial in dense or clay-heavy soils, promoting better root growth for all plants in the vicinity.

As comfrey and borage plants die back or are pruned, their leaves can be left on the soil surface to decompose, adding valuable organic matter and further enriching the soil. Borage, in particular, produces beautiful flowers that attract bees and other pollinators, beneficial for the overall health of your garden. The large leaves of comfrey can be cut and used as a nutrient-rich mulch around other plants, providing nutrients as well as suppressing weed growth.

Companion plants like comfrey and borage are excellent for soil improvement. Their deep-root systems enhance nutrient availability, improve soil structure, and contribute to the overall fertility of the garden. These plants offer a natural and sustainable way to boost the health of your garden while also supporting the growth of neighboring plants.

4. Microclimate Utilization:

Creating Microclimates through companion planting is a strategic approach that leverages the natural characteristics of plants to modify and optimize the local environment for other plants. This method can be particularly effective in managing light exposure and temperature, which are crucial factors for plant growth. By carefully selecting and positioning companion plants, gardeners can create small, controlled environments or 'microclimates' within their gardens that cater to the specific needs of various plants.

Taller plants, such as sunflowers or corn, can be strategically placed to cast shade on lower-growing, heat-sensitive varieties. This is especially beneficial in areas with intense summer sun, where excessive exposure can stress plants, leading to issues like bolting in lettuce or spinach.

The shade provided by taller plants helps in maintaining cooler soil temperatures and reduces evaporation, thus conserving moisture. This can be crucial for the health of plants that thrive in cooler conditions or require consistent soil moisture.

Tall plants can also act as windbreaks, sheltering more delicate plants from strong winds that can cause physical damage or dry out the soil quickly. In dry climates, creating shaded areas can help maintain higher humidity levels around certain plants, reducing water stress and potentially improving growth.

It's important to select companion plants that are compatible in terms of their water, nutrient, and space requirements. For example, pairing deep-rooted plants with shallow-rooted ones can prevent competition for nutrients at the same soil depth.

Creating microclimates through companion planting is an effective way to enhance the growing conditions within your garden. By using taller plants to provide shade and protection, gardeners can create areas that cater to the specific needs of heat-sensitive plants, thus promoting a more diverse and productive garden ecosystem.

Observation and Adaptation are key principles in the art of gardening, enabling gardeners to respond effectively to the ever-changing dynamics of their garden environment. By closely monitoring how different areas of the garden react to varying weather conditions, gardeners can make informed decisions about adjusting their plantings to optimize growth and health.

Keep a keen eye on how specific areas of your garden are affected by weather elements like sunlight, rain, wind, and temperature fluctuations. Some areas may receive more sun or shade, be more prone to drying out, or be more protected from wind. Use these observations to adapt your planting strategy. For instance, if a particular section of your garden receives intense afternoon sun, it might be better suited for sun-loving plants, while shaded areas can be utilized for plants that thrive in cooler conditions.

Adjust your watering practices based on how different garden areas retain or lose moisture. Areas exposed to full sun may require more frequent watering compared to shaded areas. In areas susceptible to strong winds or frost, consider implementing protective measures such as windbreaks or frost cloths.

Keeping a garden journal documenting weather conditions and plant responses can be invaluable for future planning and adjustments. Regularly walking through your garden to observe and note changes allows for timely interventions and adaptations.

The practice of observation and adaptation in gardening is a dynamic process of learning and responding to the unique conditions of your garden. By understanding how different areas react to weather and adjusting your plantings accordingly, you can create a garden that is not only resilient but also thriving in harmony with its natural surroundings.

5. Advanced Pest and Disease Control:

Trap Cropping on a Larger Scale is an innovative and eco-friendly pest management strategy that utilizes specific plants to attract pests away from your main crops. By planting these 'trap crops' around the garden's perimeter or interspersed between rows, gardeners can effectively safeguard their primary plants, ensuring healthier growth and better yields.

Positioning trap crops around the edges of your garden creates a first line of defense against pests. For example, planting nasturtiums to attract aphids away from vegetables or marigolds to deter nematodes.

Placing trap crops between the rows of your main crops can intercept pests, preventing them from reaching your valuable plants. This method can be particularly effective against pests that move slowly or are less likely to fly.

The choice of trap crop should be based on the specific pests prevalent in your area and the main crops you are growing. For instance, mustard plants can attract caterpillars away from brassicas like broccoli and cabbage.

Select trap crops known to be more attractive to pests than your main crops. The goal is to make these plants the preferred choice for pests, drawing them away from your primary plants.

Trap cropping is a sustainable approach to pest management, reducing the need for chemical pesticides. This not only benefits the environment but also ensures healthier produce for consumption. Trap crops can also serve as an early warning system, indicating the presence of pests before they reach your main crops, allowing for timely interventions.

Trap cropping can be effectively combined with other organic pest control methods, such as biological controls or barrier methods, to create a comprehensive pest management system.

Implementing trap cropping on a larger scale is a proactive and environmentally friendly approach to protecting your garden. By strategically using certain plants to attract pests, you can significantly reduce the damage to your main crops and promote a more sustainable and productive garden ecosystem.

Beneficial Insect Attraction: attracting beneficial insects through the strategic planting of certain flowers and herbs is a cornerstone of natural pest control in gardening. This approach, known as creating an insectary garden, involves cultivating plants that lure beneficial insects, such as ladybugs, lacewings, bees, and hoverflies, which play a crucial role in controlling pest populations and pollinating plants.

Incorporate a diverse range of flowering plants and herbs in your garden. Different beneficial insects are attracted to different types of flowers, so a variety ensures a wider range of helpful insects. For example, lavender and yarrow attract ladybugs, while dill and fennel are favorites of lacewings.

These insect-attracting plants not only aid in pest control but also add beauty and fragrance to your garden. Flowering plants like calendula and cosmos provide splashes of color, while herbs like basil and thyme offer culinary benefits.

By attracting beneficial insects, you reduce the need for chemical pesticides, fostering a more natural and balanced garden ecosystem. Many of these insects are also pollinators, contributing to the health and productivity of your fruit and vegetable crops.

Position these plants throughout the garden, especially near crops that are prone to pest issues. This proximity ensures that beneficial insects are present right where they are needed most. Choose plants that bloom at different times throughout the growing season to ensure a constant presence of beneficial insects.

Attracting beneficial insects through a variety of flowers and herbs is an effective, environmentally friendly way to manage pests in the garden. This method not only enhances natural pest control but also contributes to creating a vibrant, productive, and ecologically balanced gardening space.

6. Companion Planting for Perennials:

Long-Term Companions: Companion planting for perennial plants and trees is a long-term investment in the health and productivity of your garden. By thoughtfully pairing perennials with compatible companions, you can create symbiotic relationships that benefit your garden year after year. A classic example is planting chives around rose bushes, which offers multiple benefits and exemplifies the potential of this approach.

Chives, when planted near rose bushes, can help deter common pests like aphids. The strong scent of chives acts as a natural repellent, reducing pest infestations and the need for chemical pesticides. The presence of companion plants like chives can also contribute to the overall health of rose bushes. They can improve soil quality and provide a more aesthetically pleasing garden environment. Perennial companions grow and develop together over the years, forming a stable ecosystem. This stability can lead to improved resilience and growth for both plants.

It's important to pair perennials that have similar needs in terms of light, water, and soil conditions. This ensures that one plant doesn't outcompete or negatively impact the other. Ensure that companions are spaced in a way that allows both plants enough room to grow without crowding. Over time, perennials can become quite large, and adequate space is crucial for their development.

Incorporate a variety of flowering perennials, herbs, and shrubs to attract beneficial insects and birds, creating a dynamic and interactive garden ecosystem. When planning a perennial garden with companions, think about how the plants will grow and interact over several years, not just in the immediate season.

Companion planting for perennial plants and trees is a strategy that enhances garden health and beauty over the long term. It offers a sustainable way to manage pests, improve plant growth, and create a stable and diverse garden environment that evolves beautifully year after year.

Guild Planting is an ecological gardening practice that involves grouping various plants around a central species, such as a fruit tree or shrub, to create a mutually beneficial ecosystem. This method mimics natural ecosystems and focuses on the symbiotic relationships between different plants, offering advantages like pest control, improved microclimate, and enhanced soil quality.

Start with a central plant, typically a fruit tree or shrub, which forms the guild's focal point. Surround it with a variety of other plants that offer complementary benefits. For example, leguminous plants can fix nitrogen in the soil, benefiting the central fruit tree. Include plants that naturally repel pests or attract beneficial insects. For instance, marigolds or lavender can deter pests, reducing the need for chemical interventions.

A guild typically includes ground covers, herbaceous plants, shrubs, and sometimes vines, each occupying different vertical and horizontal layers. This diversity creates a rich habitat and helps to utilize space efficiently. Ground-cover plants can protect the soil from erosion, retain moisture, and suppress weeds. Deep-rooted companions can help break up compact soil and bring up nutrients.

Plant guilds support a wider range of wildlife, from pollinators to beneficial predators, contributing to ecological balance. Guild planting promotes a self-sustaining environment that requires less maintenance and inputs over time, as the plants support each other.

Guild planting around fruit trees or shrubs is a holistic approach that harnesses the strengths of various plants to create a thriving, self-sustaining mini-ecosystem. This method not only enhances the health and productivity of individual plants but also contributes to a more biodiverse, resilient, and ecologically balanced garden.

7. Precision Watering Techniques:

Drip Irrigation: Implementing a drip irrigation system in a companion garden is an efficient and precise method to meet the diverse water needs of different plants. This targeted watering approach delivers water directly to the base of each plant, minimizing waste and ensuring that each plant receives the exact amount of water it requires.

COMPANION PLANTING FOR BEGINNERS

Drip irrigation allows water to slowly drip to the roots of plants, providing a steady supply of moisture directly where it's needed. This reduces evaporation and runoff, ensuring more water reaches the plant roots. In a companion garden, plants with varying water requirements are grown together. A drip system can be adjusted to deliver more water to thirstier plants and less to those with lower water needs, ensuring optimal hydration for each plant.

This system is highly water-efficient, making it ideal for areas with water scarcity or for gardeners aiming to conserve water. By minimizing water contact with foliage, drip irrigation lowers the risk of leaf diseases that can occur with overhead watering. Efficient watering leads to healthier plants and can improve both growth rates and yields. Plants receive a consistent water supply, which is crucial for their development.

Drip irrigation systems can be relatively easy to install and can be adapted to any garden size or shape. The system can be expanded or modified as your garden grows or changes, making it a versatile solution for long-term garden development.

A drip irrigation system is a highly effective and sustainable watering solution for companion gardens. Its ability to deliver water precisely and efficiently to a variety of plants with different needs makes it an invaluable tool for gardeners seeking to optimize plant health and water usage.

Mulching Strategies: Mulching is a key strategy in successful gardening, particularly effective in companion planting setups where plants with varying needs share space. Organic mulches like straw, wood chips, or leaf litter play a critical role in retaining soil moisture, regulating temperature, and even adding nutrients back into the soil. The type and amount of mulch used can be tailored to suit the specific requirements of different companion plants in your garden.

Mulch helps maintain soil moisture by reducing evaporation, a crucial benefit during dry periods. This consistent moisture availability is key for plant health and productivity. It acts as an insulating layer, keeping the soil cooler in hot weather and warmer during cold spells. This stable environment can be particularly beneficial for young or sensitive plants. Mulch inhibits weed

COMPANION PLANTING FOR BEGINNERS

growth, reducing competition for nutrients. As organic mulches decompose, they enrich the soil with nutrients, improving its structure and fertility.

Different plants benefit from different mulching techniques. For example, leafy greens might thrive with a lighter mulch that allows more temperature fluctuation, while more robust plants like tomatoes may benefit from a thicker layer that better retains moisture. Be mindful of the water and air needs of your plants. Some plants prefer drier conditions and can be negatively impacted by too much moisture retention.

Apply mulch around the base of plants, leaving some space around the stem to prevent rot or pest issues. The thickness can vary based on the plant's needs and the local climate conditions. Adjust the mulching strategy with the changing seasons – lighter during spring and fall, and heavier during the intense heat of summer or the cold of winter.

Implementing strategic mulching practices in a companion planting garden can significantly enhance plant health and productivity. By choosing the right type of organic mulch and applying it in a way that aligns with the needs of your companion plants, you can create a more resilient, healthy, and productive garden.

By implementing these intermediate strategies, you'll be able to cultivate a garden that's not only productive but also a resilient and sustainable ecosystem. These tips and tricks will enhance your gardening experience, bringing you closer to the intricacies of nature's interactions within your garden.

Incorporating Cover Crops in Home Gardens

Cover crops, often an overlooked aspect of home gardening, play a crucial role in enhancing soil health, controlling pests, and improving overall garden productivity. Now we delve into how incorporating cover crops can be a game-changer in your companion gardening strategy, offering a sustainable approach to maintaining and improving your garden ecosystem.

COMPANION PLANTING FOR BEGINNERS

Cover crops are plants grown primarily to benefit the soil rather than for consumption. They can prevent soil erosion, improve soil fertility, suppress weeds, and enhance water retention. Common cover crops include legumes (like clover and vetch), grasses (such as ryegrass and barley), and brassicas (like mustard and radishes).

Leguminous cover crops, such as clover and alfalfa, have the unique ability to fix atmospheric nitrogen into the soil, enriching it for future plantings. Planting these crops as part of your rotation, especially before nitrogen-hungry plants like tomatoes, can naturally boost soil fertility.

Grasses and cereals have deep root systems that can break up compacted soil, improving aeration and drainage. These crops also add organic matter to the soil when tilled in, enhancing its structure and nutrient content.

Dense cover crops can outcompete weeds for space and resources, reducing the need for herbicides. Some cover crops, like mustard, act as biofumigants, suppressing soil-borne pests and diseases.

Flowering cover crops provide food and habitat for beneficial insects, including pollinators and natural pest predators. Incorporate flowering cover crops like buckwheat or phacelia to boost your garden's ecological diversity.

Choose cover crops based on your climate, soil type, and specific garden needs. Some cover crops are better for certain seasons or soil conditions. Sow cover crops during your garden's off-season or as a part of crop rotation. They can be sown between rows or as green manure before planting your main crops.

Before they set seed, mow down or till cover crops into the soil. This adds organic matter and nutrients back into the soil. For a no-till approach, cut or roll the cover crops to create a natural mulch layer that will decompose over time.

Incorporating cover crops into your companion gardening plan offers a range of benefits, from improving soil health to creating a more balanced and sustainable garden ecosystem. With thoughtful selection and management, cover crops can significantly contribute to the long-term success and vitality of your garden.

Organic and Sustainable Practices

In companion gardening, adopting organic and sustainable practices not only contributes to the health of your garden but also to the well-being of the environment. In this part of the book we focuse on integrating these practices into your companion gardening strategy, ensuring that your garden thrives in a way that is both ecologically responsible and sustainable over the long term.

Create and use compost to add vital organic matter and nutrients to your soil, enhancing its fertility and structure. Opt for organic fertilizers like bone meal, blood meal, or fish emulsion to provide additional nutrients to your plants without the use of chemicals.

Employ drip irrigation systems for efficient water usage, ensuring water is delivered directly to the plant roots where it's needed most. Collect rainwater in barrels or tanks and use it for watering your garden, reducing your reliance on tap water.

Utilize natural predators like ladybugs for aphid control or introduce beneficial nematodes for soil-dwelling pests. Make use of homemade or commercially available organic pest repellents that are less harmful to the environment and beneficial insects.

Plant a variety of flowering herbs and plants to attract bees, butterflies, and other pollinators essential for garden health and productivity. Refrain from using pesticides that can harm pollinators, opting for natural pest control methods instead.

Rotate crops annually to prevent soil nutrient depletion and disrupt cycles of pests and diseases. Change companion plant pairings each season to keep the soil nutrient-rich and to reduce the risk of disease.

COMPANION PLANTING FOR BEGINNERS

Choose garden tools and materials that are sustainably sourced or made from recycled materials. Regularly maintain and repair garden tools to extend their lifespan, reducing waste and the need for replacements.

Cultivate a diverse range of plants to create a balanced ecosystem that supports a variety of wildlife and beneficial insects. Leave some areas of your garden a little wild to provide natural habitats for beneficial creatures.

By embracing these organic and sustainable practices, you create a garden that not only yields abundant harvests but also contributes positively to the environment. This approach to gardening ensures that your impact is beneficial, supporting a healthier planet while enjoying the fruits of your labor.

Harvesting and Utilizing Your Garden

The culmination of all your planning, planting, and caring comes to fruition in this rewarding phase: harvesting and utilizing your garden. This chapter, is dedicated to guiding you through the final, yet ongoing, stage of your gardening journey. It's about reaping the rewards of your companion garden, a process that is as satisfying as it is delicious and beneficial.

Harvesting is more than just the act of picking fruits and vegetables; it's a skill that involves timing, techniques, and understanding the best uses for your produce. In this chapter, we will explore the nuances of harvesting – knowing when your crops are at their peak, how to harvest them for maximum yield and quality, and ways to utilize your garden's bounty in your kitchen and beyond.

We'll cover:

- •**Best Practices for Harvesting:** Tips and techniques for harvesting different types of crops, ensuring you get the most out of your garden while preserving the health of the plants.

- •**Recipes and Uses for Your Produce:** Creative and delicious ways to enjoy the fruits of your labor, from simple salads to gourmet dishes.

- **Preservation and Storage Tips:** Methods to extend the life of your harvest, whether it's through canning, freezing, drying, or other preservation techniques.

This chapter will not only provide practical guidance but also inspire you to celebrate every harvest from your companion garden. Whether it's a handful of fresh herbs or a bumper crop of tomatoes, each harvest carries the satisfaction of a job well done and the joy of a connection to the earth.

As we delve into the world of harvesting and utilizing your garden, you'll discover that the end of the growing season is just the beginning of enjoying and sharing your garden's bounty.

Best Practices for Harvesting

Harvesting your garden's produce is a gratifying experience, marking the success of your companion planting efforts. However, correct harvesting techniques are crucial for maximizing yield, ensuring quality, and maintaining the health of your plants. This subchapter provides best practices for harvesting various types of crops, helping you gather your produce at its peak.

1. Timing is Key:

Understanding ripeness is essential in harvesting crops at the peak of their flavor and nutritional value. Each type of crop has specific indicators of ripeness, and recognizing these signs ensures that you enjoy your garden's produce at its best. For instance, tomatoes, a common and beloved garden staple, provide clear visual and tactile cues when they're ready to be picked. Tomatoes are typically ready to harvest when they've reached their full color, which can vary from deep red to yellow, orange, or even purple, depending on the variety. The uniformity of color is a reliable indicator of ripeness. Ripe tomatoes will feel slightly soft to the touch. If a tomato still feels firm, it might need a few more days to ripen fully.

Most fruits and vegetables show color changes as they ripen. Peppers transition from green to red, yellow, or orange, and eggplants attain a glossy sheen. Apart from tomatoes, other crops also change in texture. Cucumbers should be firm but not hard, and squash should not feel too soft. Some vegetables, like zucchini and beans, are best harvested when they reach a specific size - not too small but before they become overly large and tough.

Harvesting at the right time ensures the best flavor and nutritional content. Overripe produce can be less flavorful and have a less desirable texture. Many plants will continue to produce more fruit if the ripe ones are harvested regularly. This is particularly true for tomatoes, peppers, and beans.

Understanding the signs of ripeness for each type of crop in your garden is crucial for enjoying the fruits of your labor. Whether it's the deep, uniform color of a ripe tomato or the firmness of a cucumber, these indicators help you harvest your produce at the optimal time for taste, texture, and nutritional value.

Morning Harvest: Harvesting in the morning is a practice seasoned gardeners often recommend, particularly for leafy greens and herbs. The rationale behind this timing lies in the plant's natural rhythms and responses to the environment. In the morning, plants are at their peak in terms of hydration and sugar content, having rejuvenated overnight.

Plants accumulate sugars overnight, which means their sugar content is highest in the early hours. This results in a sweeter, more flavorful taste, especially noticeable in leafy greens and herbs. Due to cooler temperatures and less exposure to sunlight, plants harvested in the morning tend to be crisper and more hydrated. This is particularly beneficial for leafy greens, which can wilt in the heat of the day. Produce picked in the morning generally has a longer shelf life. The cooler temperatures reduce the rate of respiration and water loss in the plants, keeping them fresher for longer after being harvested.

Plan your gardening activities so that harvesting can be done in the early hours, before the day heats up. Morning-harvested produce is at its best for immediate consumption. However, if you need to store them, proper refrigeration is key to maintaining their freshness. While morning is generally the best time to harvest, ensure that your plants are well-watered the day before, particularly in dry weather conditions, to maximize their hydration.

Harvesting in the morning can significantly enhance the quality of your garden produce. The higher sugar content, optimal freshness, and extended shelf life are compelling reasons to adopt this practice, especially for crops like leafy greens and herbs, which are particularly sensitive to the day's heat and light.

2. Gentle Handling:

Avoid Bruising: Handling your produce with care is crucial to maintain its quality and longevity post-harvest. Bruising or damage can occur easily and not only affects the appearance of fruits and vegetables but can also hasten spoilage. To minimize this risk, it's essential to be gentle when picking your produce.

Using garden scissors or pruners is a highly effective way to harvest. This method is preferable to pulling or twisting fruits and vegetables off by hand, which can cause tearing or damage to both the produce and the plant. Clean cuts made by scissors or pruners help ensure the plant remains healthy and capable of continued growth and production. Gentle handling and proper harvesting tools are simple yet impactful practices that help preserve the quality of your garden bounty.

Harvesting Technique: Mastering the correct harvesting technique for different types of produce is essential for maintaining the integrity and health of both the fruit and the plant. For root vegetables and fruits like tomatoes or peppers, specific methods ensure a successful harvest.

Harvesting Root Vegetables:

Gently loosen the soil around the base of root vegetables like carrots, beets, or radishes. This can be done with a garden fork or spade, taking care not to damage the root. Once the soil is loosened, grasp the base of the plant near the root and pull gently. The vegetable should come out smoothly without excessive force, which could damage the plant or break the root.

Harvesting Fruits:

When harvesting fruits like tomatoes or peppers, hold the fruit in your hand and twist it gently. The goal is to detach the fruit from the stem cleanly, without pulling hard enough to damage the plant or the fruit. A clean twist ensures the stem and remaining plant are not harmed, allowing for continued growth and future production.

General Harvesting Tips:

Harvest fruits and vegetables when they have reached the ideal stage of ripeness. This varies by plant but is typically indicated by color, size, and firmness. Regularly harvesting plants encourages more production. For example, picking tomatoes when ripe stimulates the plant to produce more fruit.

Harvesting herbs requires a careful approach to ensure their continued growth and to preserve their flavor and aroma. The right technique varies slightly depending on the type of herb, but there are general guidelines that apply to most. Harvest herbs early in the morning after the dew has dried but before the sun is at its peak. This is when their essential oils are most concentrated, ensuring the best flavor and aroma. Ideally, harvest herbs before they flower, as flowering can change the flavor of the leaves.

Harvesting Technique: Use sharp scissors or pruning shears to make clean cuts. This helps the plant heal quickly and continue growing. Harvest up to one-third of the plant at a time. This leaves enough foliage for the plant to continue photosynthesizing and growing. For many herbs, it's best to cut from the top. This encourages new growth and can help the plant become bushier.

Handle herbs gently to avoid bruising their delicate leaves. Use herbs fresh for the best flavor, or preserve them through drying or freezing for later use.

COMPANION PLANTING FOR BEGINNERS

Specific Considerations for Common Herbs:

Basil: Pinch off the tops to encourage a bushier plant. Regular harvesting prevents the plant from becoming leggy.

Mint: Cut stems just above a leaf node or junction to encourage fuller growth.

Rosemary and Thyme: These woody herbs can be cut back quite a bit, as they will regrow from the woodier stem parts.

Harvesting herbs in the right way and at the right time is key to maximizing their flavor and ensuring the plants remain productive. Regular and careful pruning not only provides you with fresh herbs for your culinary needs but also contributes to the health and longevity of your herb plants.

Regular Harvesting:

Regular harvesting encourages plants to produce more. For example, picking beans and peas frequently can stimulate further pod production. Overripe fruits and vegetables can attract pests and may lead to a decline in plant productivity.

Understanding Plant Recovery:

Some plants, like leafy greens, can be harvested multiple times. Ensure you leave enough foliage for the plant to recover and continue growing. Harvest outer leaves or sections of plants like lettuce and kale, leaving the inner part to continue growing.

Harvesting Root Crops:

Harvesting root crops such as carrots, beets, and turnips requires a delicate balance of timing and technique to ensure that the vegetables are at their best both in terms of size and flavor. The process begins with assessing the readiness of the crop and is followed by careful extraction from the soil.

Before harvesting, it's essential to ensure that the soil is not overly compacted. Hard soil can make harvesting difficult and may damage the crops. Gently use a garden fork to loosen the soil around the root crops. This step is crucial to avoid breaking or damaging the roots during extraction. Insert the fork into the soil at a safe distance from the crop to avoid piercing the vegetables.

Carefully brush away some soil at the top of the root crop to check its size. This can usually be done by hand or with a small tool. Harvest the crop when it has reached the desired size. This varies depending on the type of vegetable and personal preference. Generally, root crops should be harvested before they become overly large, as they can become tough and woody.

Harvesting Technique: Once the soil is loosened, grasp the base of the plant's stem and pull gently. If the vegetable does not come out easily, use the garden fork to further loosen the soil. It's important to handle the vegetables carefully to prevent bruising or damage, which can affect both the storage life and quality of the root crop. Shake off any excess soil and rinse the vegetables gently. However, for storage purposes, some gardeners recommend leaving the soil on until you're ready to use the vegetables, as this can sometimes help them last longer.

Harvesting root crops is a satisfying culmination of the gardening process. With the right techniques, you can enjoy fresh, flavorful vegetables from your garden. The key is to be gentle and patient, allowing you to reap the full benefits of your gardening efforts.

6. Fruit and Berry Harvesting:

Harvesting fruits and berries from your garden is a delightful and rewarding experience, marking the culmination of months of careful tending. The key to successful fruit and berry harvesting lies in recognizing the right time to pick them and using techniques that ensure the health of the plant remains intact.

Identifying Ripe Fruits and Berries: Ripe fruits typically reach full color and develop a strong, characteristic aroma. For instance, apples and pears should have their full, species-specific coloration and a fragrant smell. Ripe fruits and berries generally come off the plant easily. Berries like strawberries, blueberries, or raspberries should detach with a gentle pull. This is a clear indicator that they are ready for harvest. If unsure, a taste test can be the best indicator. Ripe fruits are usually at their peak of sweetness and flavor.

Techniques for Harvesting: Handle fruits and berries gently to avoid bruising. Use your fingers to pick berries rather than grabbing handfuls, and be careful not to squeeze fruits as you check for ripeness. When picking heavier fruits like apples or pears, support the branch with one hand while picking the fruit with the other. This prevents undue strain on the branch, protecting the plant from damage.

Post-Harvest Care: Many fruits and berries are best enjoyed fresh, but they can also be stored, canned, or frozen. Process them as soon as possible after harvesting for the best quality. Inspect the fruits for signs of pests or diseases. Prompt removal of affected fruits can prevent the spread to healthy ones.

Considerations for Specific Fruits: Harvesting stone fruits and citrus fruits requires an understanding of their unique ripeness indicators to ensure you pick them at the best possible time for flavor and texture. Each type of fruit has specific cues that signal it's ready to be harvested.

Stone Fruits – Peaches, Plums, and Similar: For stone fruits such as peaches and plums, the key indicator of ripeness is a slight give in the flesh. Gently press the skin with your thumb; if it yields slightly, it's likely ripe. This softness indicates that the fruit is juicy and ready to eat. Look for a deep, rich color that is uniform across the fruit. A ripe stone fruit will also emit a sweet and fragrant aroma. Ripe stone fruits will come away from the tree with a gentle twist. If you have to pull hard, the fruit may not be ready. Stone fruits tend to deteriorate quickly after ripening, so plan to consume or process them soon after picking.

Citrus Fruits – Oranges, Lemons, Limes, and Others: Citrus fruits typically show a distinct color change when ripe. Oranges turn bright orange, lemons a vivid yellow, and limes a deep green. It's important to note that the color change should be complete, as citrus fruits do not continue to ripen once picked. A ripe citrus fruit will feel firm but not hard and will have a certain heft indicating juiciness. For some citrus fruits, the texture of the skin can change, becoming smoother as the fruit ripens. If possible, taste a fruit before harvesting in bulk. Citrus fruits should have the right balance of sweetness and acidity when ripe.

General Harvesting Tips: Regularly check your fruit trees as the harvesting season approaches. Ripeness can sometimes occur quickly, and the window for optimal harvesting can be brief. For taller trees, use appropriate harvesting tools like fruit pickers to reach higher branches without damaging the tree.

Understanding these specific ripeness cues for stone and citrus fruits is crucial for harvesting them at their peak. This not only ensures the best taste and quality but also reduces waste due to overripe or unripe fruits being picked.

Fruit and berry harvesting requires a careful approach, with attention to the ripeness indicators and gentle handling to protect both the produce and the plant. The joy of consuming freshly picked fruits, bursting with flavor, is one of the great rewards of gardening, and proper harvesting techniques ensure this joy is maximized.

By following these best practices, you ensure that your harvest is not only abundant but also of the highest quality. Remember, the way you harvest is as important as how you grow, and thoughtful harvesting practices can significantly impact the health and productivity of your garden.

Conclusion

As we reach the conclusion of "Companion Gardening for Beginners," it's time to reflect on the journey we've embarked upon together. From the initial steps of understanding companion planting to the advanced techniques and community engagements, this book has been a comprehensive guide, aiming to equip you with the knowledge and skills necessary to create a thriving and sustainable garden.

In this final chapter, we look back on the key concepts covered, reinforce the importance of patience and continuous learning in gardening, and consider the broader impact of your gardening practice on the environment and your community. Gardening is not just a hobby; it's a journey of discovery, growth, and connection to the natural world.

Let's take a moment to celebrate the knowledge you've gained, the skills you've developed, and the journey ahead as you continue to cultivate your garden and grow as a gardener.

Continuing Your Gardening Journey

As you close this book, your journey in the world of companion gardening does not end; rather, it evolves. Gardening is a continuous learning process filled with ongoing discoveries and daily joys. This subchapter is dedicated to encouraging you in your future gardening endeavors and to reminding you that every day in the garden is an opportunity to grow not just your plants but also your experience and knowledge.

Be bold in experimenting with different plant pairings. Each season presents an opportunity to explore new combinations and see what works best in your garden. Keep a gardening journal to track your observations and learnings. This record can be an invaluable tool for understanding what works best in your unique gardening environment.

Gardening is an ever-evolving craft. Stay curious and continue to educate yourself through books, workshops, and interactions with other gardeners. Follow gardening blogs, podcasts, and social media channels to stay up-to-date with the latest gardening trends and techniques.

As you gain more experience, share your knowledge with others. Whether it's through mentoring, community projects, or online forums, your insights can be valuable to fellow gardeners. Continue to build and nurture relationships within the gardening community. These connections can provide support, inspiration, and camaraderie.

Recognize the positive impact your gardening practices have on the environment, from supporting pollinators to improving soil health. Take time to appreciate the personal growth and satisfaction that gardening brings. Whether it's the peace of tending to your plants or the joy of a successful harvest, gardening is a rewarding endeavor.

Each season, take time to plan your garden, considering what worked in the past and what new challenges you might want to tackle. As you become more confident, consider expanding your garden. This could mean increasing its size, trying more challenging plants, or exploring new gardening styles.

Remember, your gardening journey is uniquely yours. It's a path of discovery, filled with the wonders of nature and the satisfaction of nurturing life. Keep growing, keep learning, and most importantly, keep enjoying every moment in your garden.

Made in United States
Troutdale, OR
04/27/2024

19497456R00060